HAPPY WORK
HAPPY LIFE
AN INSIDE JOB

Humorous work stories of how the healing power of pets saved my sanity

DONNA FULLER

Copyright © 2015

Happy Work. Happy Life. An Inside Job.

Donna Fuller

All rights reserved. Although the author and publisher have made every effort to ensure that the information in this book was correct at time of going to press, the author and publisher do not assume and hereby disclaim any liability to any party for any loss, damage, or disruption caused by errors or omissions, whether such errors or omissions result from negligence, accident, or any other cause.

Acme and Baskerville Old Face fonts used with permission from Microsoft.

ISBN-13: 978-0692502907 (Fuller Humor)

ISBN-10: 692502904

To Maverick

Thank you for your strong work ethic.
Thank you for enduring job security.
Thank you for your military service.
Thank you for teaching me about life, liberty and patriotism.
Thank you for taking ah-mazing care of our critters. You are the best pet parent. It is your finest quality.
Thank you for toughing it out while I got my act together. Lord knows, being married to me has been the hardest job you'll ever have.
You deserve a promotion, raise and a medal.

To anyone who has ever held a meaningless, thankless or even fabulous job.
And to anyone who has ever been fired.
You are my people.
This book is for you.

This book uses a Large Marge typeface.
This is because the author wants
to be able to read her own book.

I hope this book adds value to your life

I hope it makes you think

I hope it makes you feel better

I hope it motivates you to move forward and move mountains

At least, move off the couch!

But most of all, I hope you giggle through the process

CONTENTS

PROLOGUE... ix
OFFICIAL BEAN PICKER 1
GARAGE SALE GURU 5
JAILER 13
FORREST GUMP 21
ICE CREAM QUEEN 27
CAFÉ COMEDIAN................................ 35
THE DATING CAFÉ 43
THE AU NATURAL EXPRESS 49
WEDDING PLANNER 57
WHACK-A-MOLE MACHINE 65
GOAT FARMER 75

COPY QUEEN 85
SECURITY ZONE 95
RESCUE MOM 103
WORD SMITHER 113
THE NUTTY PROFESSOR 121
WINE AMBASSADOR 131
DOG FOOD DEMONSTRATOR ... 139
DOG FOOD DIARIES 147
FOUR PAWS EDU 153
FOUR PAWS DELI 157
DOG TRAINER 163
DOG DRUG DEALER 173
JOKER 185
COMEDIC CATALYST 195
THE END 203
ACKNOWLEDGEMENTS 207
INDEX 209
ABOUT THE AUTHOR 215
CONTACT DONNA 217

PROLOGUE

Guinness World Book of Records sent me a formal letter:

Although we have do not have an *official* category for Most. Jobs. Ever; You win.

My resume is a combination of stories and lessons. And I'm warning you, it's colorful.

I sold jewelry, donuts, and beach chairs.

I delivered food, cocktails, and dentures.

I mowed right-a-ways, painted fingernails and dressed as Minnie Mouse.

I booked condos, guarded lives and scrubbed toilets.

I watched kids, pulled teeth and served beer, not at the same job.

I helped sick, broke and crabby people.

I dealt Black Jack, kept bar and sold grass, not the kind you smoke.

Yes, I've been a worker among workers several times over. But before you paint an "L" on my forehead for loser, let me say that life is a process of elimination. Of course, some days it was elimination, other days it was termination.

Still, no matter how they panned out each job was an opportunity to learn, laugh and grow.

This book is a glimpse of my on-the-job training for life. My stories and lessons are an effort to help get you to the place you were meant to be: living a thriving life.

And if I can do it, so can you.

OFFICIAL BEAN PICKER

Growing up at my house we didn't have Kool-Aid stands, we had vegetable stands. My first job was working at the vegetable stand.

Summertime swim practice ran from 5 a.m. to 8 a.m. Afterward, Mom picked me up and we raced to the farm to pick vegetables and to beat the heat. She peeled out of the parking lot before I got the car door closed. Texas summers are hot by sunrise, so by the time we got to the farm the temperature was already at blistering. We picked those veggies fast.

My Grampa Fuller had a sayin', "If a little's good, then a lot's better." He applied this motto when taking pills, while stuffing his pockets full of ketchup packets at McDonalds and when he built our garden. Our "family garden" was the size of Texas and the only shade came from a single Chinaberry tree in the middle.

We grew every kind of vegetable under that hot Texas sun and he planted enough for an army. There were tomatoes, green beans, yellow squash, cucumbers, radishes, banana peppers, bell peppers, eggplant, potatoes, and okra. I loathed picking that prickly, painful okra.

Really, I didn't like to eat or pick any of them, except for the green beans. I ate them raw, right off the vine.

To my mother, the fact that I liked to eat them gave her reason enough to make me the "Official Bean Picker." She made it *seem* like an honor, but I soon realized that nobody else wanted the job. The never-ending rows of green beans multiplied right before my eyes.

Loved eating 'em, hated picking 'em.

To pass the time, I would sing duets with Andy Gibb into my cucumber microphone. When not singing, I practiced my response to his marriage proposal.

I planned to let him down easy, explaining that our worlds were too far apart (*hellooo*...he lived in Australia). He desperately wanted to have my children, but when his relentless pleading did not sway me, he would come to accept my reasons. In the end, we would part friends although he assured me his everlasting love would never die.

Our garden was on our farm, but we lived across town in a popular neighborhood with constant traffic. Mom saw this as the perfect set up for a vegetable stand. I'd pull my kid's table and chairs onto the front yard sidewalk and by straight up noon, I was selling produce to customers like my dinner depended on it. Mom thought the sweltering Texas heat didn't bother me, but I can assure you, it did.

She armed me with Buckhorn beer boxes full of vegetables, a scale, bowls, and a Tupperware Stow-n-Go cash box filled with change. For carry out, I had a mile high stack of brown paper bags from my competitor, the Piggly Wiggly, courtesy of Grampa Fuller.

I waited for customers to stop, but this 9-year-old also flagged down complete strangers from the side of the road. I sold those fresh vegetables for 25 cents a pound as quick as I could because I wanted back inside where the temperature dipped below 100. To my dismay, when my supply ran low, mom just brought out more.

Then she'd race back inside and I heard the deadbolt turn. I realized soon enough I worked in my own sweatshop.

Mom told me the vegetable stand would help me build character and I'd learn how to count back change. All true. However, I think she just wanted some peace and quiet and the air conditioning all to herself.

I made it through the Texas heat, and the red, yellow and green vegetables. Although sales seemed good, I didn't see the financial fruits of my labor. The job taught me to tap into strengths and resources I never knew I had; a philosophy that followed me throughout all my jobs.

I didn't realize it at the time, but this job prepared me for many future positions, where I received no *on-the-job training*. I learned to take responsibility and figure things out for myself. Manning that vegetable stand required me to make the most of my natural strengths, uncover my people skills and utilize available resources, all without thinking it to death.

The reward was that my first job at the vegetable stand helped get me to the place I was meant to be: living a thriving life.

And if I can tap into my natural talents and strengths, so can you.

GARAGE SALE GURU

I don't think I knew they had *real stores* as a child because we only shopped at garage sales. In town, my mom was so well known for her second-hand shopping skills that people gave her bumper stickers that read, "I brake for garage sales!" and "Garage Sale Queen". Dad thought it sacrilege to stick *anything* on a bumper so she filed them away in her desk drawer. I suspect when no one was looking she pulled them out to admire, feeling like she'd won the Nobel Peace Prize.

On occasion, she would "dumpster dive" behind department stores early in the mornings before the garbage truck took away the treasures. Her favorite find -- a mannequin hand. When company came over, she slipped it in between the toilet seat lids to make it look like someone was climbing out. We'd wait quietly in the hallway, right outside the bathroom door, so we could hear them as they jumped out of their skin.

The peak garage sale season ran from May through August, but my mom scoured the sales year-round. She'd drop us off at school, slowing down only enough for us to jump safely out of the moving car. Then like a pit crew member, she'd scream GO! GO! GO! and peel away from the curb.

On Wednesday morning, Mom waited anxiously for the Herald-Zeitung newspaper because it contained the coveted garage sale ads for the week. Back and forth she'd pace between the kitchen and our good living room. She peered out the picture window waiting for the paper to hit the sidewalk like a junkie waiting on her dealer.

She'd hear the paper hit the sidewalk and unbolted the deadlock faster than a safe cracker. Still robed, she'd make a mad-dash across the front yard as if someone might steal her prized possession.

After clearing off the kitchen table and ordering us to "MOVE!" Mom spread out the newspaper like a treasure map and combed through every garage sale ad. Marks-A-Lot in hand, she drew a thick border around the ones fitting her criteria and a big X through the ones that didn't. She mapped out her route according to the neighborhood and then scanned for items she thought she couldn't live without. She wrote all her notes in shorthand so none of us could decipher the code because that's how she Christmas shopped.

At least once a summer we held our own massive three-family garage sale. Basically, we sold all the junk we'd accumulated from everyone else's sales.

I got to keep the proceeds from selling my stuff and I loved having money to burn. I was giddy at the thought of buying something new. Well, new-to-me anyway, because we only shopped at garage sales.

On the other hand, my brother, Bud, was a hoarder. Mom had to farm him out to a neighbor's house to play in order to clean out his closet. She'd hide his stuff in thick black contractor bags.

Once, he came home early and busted her in the middle of bagging up his belongings. He opened the sack and pulled out his toys slowly, one by one. With tears welling up in his eyes, he told her, "But, I was saving these for my children."

He was six.

Our garage sales were a huge undertaking. We spent weeks going through closets, dresser drawers and toy boxes preparing for the big day. We shared the event and cost with Mrs. Fischer, my mom's best friend.

We held the garage sales at Mrs. Fischer's house because my dad didn't want anyone knowing about our money-making operation. It didn't matter because the whole town considered my mom the go-to-gal when it came to garage sales. Mom had such a reputation that when people shopped at sales they'd call her for a price check.

We handled all pre-sale preparations behind our closed garage doors. We allowed no early lookers and even covered the garage windows with double-layered butcher paper so no one could sneak a peek. We had wall-to-wall makeshift plywood tables on saw horses and a half dozen card tables.

On the night before, we held a dry run to make sure everything flowed smoothly during the big event. We invited a few privileged neighbors to shop before opening day, but Mom guarded that guest list like a night club bouncer.

Mom passed out masking tape and markers to everyone. She let me price most of my own items, but since all I saw were dollar signs, I marked them up by 300%. After I went to bed, I'm sure she marked them back down by 295%.

We'd put the price and our initials on a piece of masking tape to keep things straight at checkout. Sometimes, hoping to add value, I'd write on a separate piece of tape "ONLY WORN TWICE!" across my favorite ratty old shirt or "RARE ITEM!" on an earring missing its mate. Even at age ten, I knew how to grab people's attention by highlighting benefits.

On sale day, by 4 a.m. we had dismantled our tables, loaded them in the truck and hauled them 2 blocks over to Mrs. Fischer's driveway. *Finer* clothing was strung between the live oak trees.

Setup began at 5 a.m. because eager buyers would camp out in front of the house by 6 a.m. We could see them waiting in their cars, trying to use their Jedi-mind tricks, willing us to "Open-Open-Open". It felt powerful making them wait. We'd chuckle amongst ourselves at how desperate they appeared, while knowing we had done the same thing ourselves the weekend before.

At 7 a.m. my mother would yell out to the cars, "It's Showtime!" and customers charged the driveway like groupies rushing a stage.

And, of course, in our family, you couldn't have a garage sale without our other side business, a vegetable stand. When I wasn't on vegetable stand duty, I walked around and kept an eye on customers.

I'd ask if they needed help, suggest some of my favorite items and try to sell them on the value. More importantly, I made sure they weren't shoplifting that 25¢ pair of jeans.

Now, the wheeling and dealing began. If it was my item, Mom would point to me and tell the customer, "You'll have to ask her." So, I would take a minute and pretend to consider whether their lowball offer justified the value of my item or not. Then, I'd act like I was doing them a favor, and say, "Oh, why not."

It felt good and a little powerful to negotiate and cut someone a deal.

At the checkout table, Mom stocked our Tupperware Stow-N-Go cash box with markers, pencils, a calculator and change. Customers used the checkout as their last attempt for haggling. I used it as my last chance to up sell items I knew they couldn't live without.

Working garage sales taught me that life is about negotiating and sales. We sell our credibility to potential employers and spouses. We negotiate payment terms, salaries, and who's going to take out the trash. Bargaining is all part of our daily lives.

Life is also about being of service to family, customers, bosses and our community. A mom serves her kids as a Taxi cab. An employee serves a customer by delivering knowledge, skills or dinner with honesty and a smile. They serve a boss by supporting the company's vision and generating profits. And a volunteer serves the community by donating time and money to support a valued cause.

I learned to wheel and deal from selling and buying at garage sales. And, that it may take some haggling, but everything in life is negotiable.

My job as a garage sale guru helped get me to the place I was meant to be: living a thriving life.

And if I can negotiate, so can you.

Everything in life is negotiable.

~ Donna Fuller

JAILER

Mrs. Fischer, my mom's garage sale partner, ran a day-care out of her home. She usually kept up to 25 kids at a time. Most of them were under the age of five. The remaining kids were older, but their parents knew they couldn't be left home alone without the possibility of burning down the house.

At lunch time, Mrs. Fischer lined up a dozen high chairs in the kitchen for the little ones. The older kids sat at the kitchen table and picnic tables strung throughout the house. She served grapes and either mayonnaise and cheese or peanut butter and honey sandwiches to everyone.

We didn't have a 3-second rule for anything that fell on the floor because nothing lasted that long. Mrs. Fisher's dog, Mutsy, or a kid quickly scarfed up anything that hit the floor. Sometimes they would share.

As soon as the first group of kids finished eating, Mrs. Fischer put them down for naps and brought in the next round. There was a kid on every bed and on every floor. When they weren't napping, they played outside, mostly unsupervised, by the fish pond.

Come to think of it, her home could be the reason we have our current childcare laws.

I loved babies, so along with Mrs. Fischer's girls, I helped watch the kids while she taught piano.

By age ten, Mrs. Fischer started pimping me out, I mean referring me out. I watched kids just long enough for their parents to catch one of their other children's games. Parents also called on me so they could make a kid-free, mad dash through the grocery store.

By age twelve, my babysitting gigs and income increased *substantially*. My most memorable family had a kid named Ryan. He made Dennis the Menace look like a saint.

Sitting for Ryan required attention and skill, and every gig at his house was an adventure. And not the good kind of adventure. Whoever babysat Ryan over the weekend gave the lowdown to the other sitters come Monday morning at school.

He fought nap time so hard, kicking and screaming, that it took his brother, sister and me to drag him to his room. Once I got him in there, I had to lock the padlock on the outside of his door. His parents installed the lock after Ryan figured out how to escape by knocking the pins out of the door hinges with his Fisher Price Tool Set.

Once he went to sleep he slept like a hibernating grizzly bear, but getting him there was like fighting one.

During Ryan's meltdowns I could hear him slamming his Erector Set and Tonka Trucks against the walls. Then he cried and screamed like he was dying. I learned it was just a ploy to get out. Once, I felt sorry for him, so I opened the door slightly to check on him. Ryan saw daylight, barreled over me and ran straight for the front yard.

That boy was the strongest four-year-old I ever met and he could take me down.

One evening Ryan refused to go to sleep and I heard him jumping on his bed. I thought he'd eventually wear out, but after 2 hours of jumping and wailing, I went to his door to say for the hundredth time, "GO TO SLEEP!"

I opened the door to find him in midair.

Just as I yelled, "Quit jumping or your gonna break your...," the slats busted in two and his double-sized bed crashed to the floor.

Other than being in shock he looked okay. "I told you," was my only remark. Then I shut off the lights, closed the door and locked the padlock. I didn't hear a word out of him the rest of the night.

Once, while making grilled cheese sandwiches for the kids I heard a strange noise coming from the garage. I looked into the living room and saw the other kids sitting quietly on the couch watching TV. We shot each other a look of panic as we realized Ryan was M.I.A.

We ran to the back door. We saw Ryan push the automatic garage door opener and race towards the closing door. Clearing the sensor, he laid himself down face-up on the concrete floor waiting to see if the door would close on his skull or stop just inches above.

By age thirteen, I had built quite the reputation: nobody died on my watch, I was easy to work with and my prices were fair. Customers began spreading the word that I was the sitter to hire.

People booked me on New Year's Eve for the following New Year's Eve and I always had a 6-month waiting list. When I realized some of my parent customers were going out with my other parent customers I got resourceful. I offered to watch all the family's kids together at one house and gave everyone a *slight* discounted rate.

They loved me for it.

And, like Mrs. Fischer I started pimping out, I mean referring out, my other trusted babysitter friends. Early on I learned that making friends and spreading the wealth with my competition was a win-win for everyone. And the other babysitters returned the favor.

Soon we were all rolling in the 75 cents an hour dough, which was big money back then!

Kids were happy. Babysitters were happy. And parent customers were very happy.

Now, if only I had known about referral fees...

For the first time, I saw the fruits of my labor! It felt great to have instant cash in my pocket. I bought my first stereo with AM/FM radio, turntable, and 8-track player, all for $130 from JC Penny's. I paid for church camps and plane trips on Southwest Airlines to visit family in the Rio Grande Valley.

It felt great to be self-supporting, well as much as you can be at age fourteen.

I got real satisfaction in getting paid for a job well done and knowing I earned the money using my talents and gifts. Self-sufficiency is empowering. Self-sufficiency is confidence. Self-sufficiency is freedom.

At 16, thinking the parents would never find out, I snuck a cold beer from the fridge at one of my babysitting gigs. Pretty soon I found beer and boys much more appealing than watching kids. Word got out and after that, requests for my services came to a screeching halt.

I learned many lessons during my babysitting days. Yes, some of them were hard, but they made an unforgettable impact. I learned there were consequences for my actions. My choices cost me my job. My choices cost me my reputation. But most of all, my choices cost me my self-respect.

I also tapped into my natural strengths and resources. I worked smarter, not harder. I created a win-win system that made the kids, my sitter "colleagues" and parent customers very happy.

And I had my first taste of self-sufficiency which gave me empowerment, confidence, and freedom. I carried those skills with me into other jobs, building a foundation for continued success.

My job as a jailer, I mean babysitter, helped get me to the place I was meant to be: living a thriving life.

And if I can work smarter, so can you.

Self-sufficiency is confidence.

Self-sufficiency is empowering.

Self-sufficiency is freedom.

~ Donna Fuller

FORREST GUMP

The summer after 2nd grade, I asked my parents if I could join the swim team. I wanted to hang out at the pool with my two friends, Julie and Alison, and to get away from my parents. I had no idea competition would be required.

The first day of swim practice, Julie and I horsed around in the pool and almost drowned each other. Luckily, Alison jumped in and pulled us to safety.

Practice lasted two hours, twice a day. And eventually, I started competing. I loved being in the water. I loved being a Gruene Dolphin.

Only one problem-I stunk. The few ribbons I won were like 7th place out of 7... 8th place out of 7... I don't think I ever made "B time." You swimmers know what I'm talking about.

In fact, the minute that gun went off at the starting block, I would have waved them off saying, "Ya'll go ahead." But, because my dad was President of the Aquatics Club and he was there...watching...**all-the-time**, I *had* to dive in and *swim.*

When I was 10, Coach Dallmann made the big announcement at our weekly covered dish supper. The Gruene Dolphins were traveling to Mexico City and would compete against the Correcaminos (the Roadrunners).

In order to raise money for the trip, we would hold a Swim-a-thon. We swimmers had to commit to swimming a certain number of laps within two hours and sell pledges.

On one hand, I didn't want to let my team down, but, on the other hand, I knew I stunk. To be on the safe side, I lowballed the number and put myself down for a measly 20 laps.

"That's it?" my mom said, rolling her eyes.

Reluctantly, I raised it to 30, even though I didn't think I had it in me to make-up the 10 lap difference.

With my lap commitment made, I started going door to door asking for pledges. Back then, parents (especially *my parents*) didn't fundraise *for* their kids. Nobody left Girl Scout cookies or Band Booster candy bars for sale in their office break room. Oh no, I was required to beat the streets, go door to door, and face possible rejection like everybody else.

My sales strategy started with cold calls to people I knew. I gave my pitch to family and friends who gladly pledged 5¢ or 10¢ a lap. My grandparents, however, upped the ante to 25¢ a lap. They probably did the math and figured at 30 laps I wouldn't break the bank.

Next, I knocked on doors all over the neighborhood asking for pledges. I would greet them politely and tell them about our cause. Then I showed them what my grandparents had pledged (why not shoot high?) and asked for their bid.

I don't remember anybody telling me no. I told them I'd collect my earnings after the Swim-a-thon. I always thanked everyone and ended my spiel with, "Pleasure doin' bidness with ya!"

The evening of our deadline I turned in a page full of 5¢, 10¢ and 25¢ pledges.

Our Swim-a-thon started out like any other day. We got in our lanes, and with clock set; we swam in circles like sharks.

I easily finished my 30 laps and thought

about getting out of the pool. Then, I thought since I'd gone this far maybe I'd just keep on going. When I hit the next 30 laps, for no particular reason, I figured I might as well just keep on going.

I had turned into Forrest Gump.

When I came up for air at the wall, they shoveled spun honey into my mouth (and all over my goggles) for energy. Each time I neared the edge, I heard Coach Dallmann and my teammates cheering me on from the side of the pool. So I just kept on going. And when I got tired, I got out. 120 laps later.

Coach Dallman threw me up on his shoulders and paraded me around the Olympic pool. The local newspaper did a write up on me. That Swim-a-thon was the proudest day of my life.

I went to collect my earnings and jaws dropped when I told them their totals had quadrupled. They acted like I had broken the bank.

Nobody, including myself, ever thought I had it in me. But that Swim-a-Thon experience proved otherwise. I quadrupled my efforts with encouragement from the sidelines. When motivated, I had more in me than I thought I did.

I learned I had drive, stamina, and perseverance. I had it in me going door to door and I had it in me as I kept on swimming. I learned when I put my mind to it, there was no stopping me.

That day I learned not to underestimate myself. Today, when I doubt my abilities - when I don't believe I have it in me - I think back to that proud moment and remind myself to keep on going.

I tell myself: I have drive. I have stamina. I have perseverance. There is nothing to stop me.

My job going door to door selling Swim-a-thon pledges helped get me to the place I was meant to be: living a thriving life.

And if I can exceed expectations, so can you.

*There is nothing
to stop you.*

~ Donna Fuller

ICE CREAM QUEEN

My first *real* job was scooping ice cream at Baskin-Robbins. The interview consisted of two questions: can you work weekdays/weekends and when can you start? I answered "Yes" and "as soon as possible" and was hired on the spot. The manager, Cindy, handed me my uniform and put me on the schedule the next day.

In 1981, we wore solid chocolate brown polyester stretch pants. The matching shirt had stylish hot pink and orange vertical stripes. They gave us trucker-style caps made of breathable mesh with a pink 31 embroidered in the middle of the crown.

The first day of work, I met the assistant

manager, James, and the rest of my co-workers who had also aced the interview. We were a motley crew, a mixture of kids I knew from school or church, all starting our first real job.

Our on-the-job training consisted of a 7-minute tour of the store. Cindy pointed out the overstock buckets of ice cream inside the walk-in freezer and showed us the instruction book on how to make everything from a vanilla shake to a Matterhorn. Her motivational speech was a one-liner, "You'll figure it out." And then she packed up her stuff and made a beeline out the door.

The next day Cindy called to say she would be taking some sick days.

James asked, "How long?"

"Eight weeks," she replied. "And if the owners call, can you cover for me?" And with that, she left 12 teenagers in charge for the rest of the summer.

We soon realized the owners knew nothing about Cindy's leave of absence. When they called, she instructed us to say she was in the bathroom, take a message and call her at home immediately. She checked in by phone every couple of weeks to gather information for her payroll reports, so she could get paid. Cindy continued to "work" from home, but we never saw her again.

Our crew became close friends and worked well together as a team. We liked our job and each other. We wanted to be there and, as a result, no one called in sick or bailed on their shift. When someone needed a day off, we jumped at the chance to cover for them.

Surprisingly, we were more dependable than some of the adults I worked with at future jobs. We reveled in our unsupervised positions and the perks of unlimited ice cream all while collecting a paycheck. We had the teenage dream job and we knew it.

The Texas summer heat brought us a steady stream of customers. During lulls, we engaged in ice cream fights or we traded ice cream for pizza with the near-by Pizza Inn. We ate and gave away more ice cream than we sold.

We tested all 31 flavors many times. Baskin-Robbins must have foreseen stretch pants as a necessary part of the uniform, because you tend to stretch when engaging in repeated daily taste tests.

We used those little pink spoons, but with everyone tasting ice cream all the time, well, that's a lot of wasted spoons! And all our lives our moms had ordered us, "Don't waste that!", so we decided to reuse our spoons. Too bad we didn't think to wash them in between taste tests.

Daiquiri Ice was my favorite. It was a pretty aqua blue color and I believed if I ate enough of it, I'd catch a buzz. The only buzz I caught was an ice cream headache.

We delighted in locking each other in the walk-in freezer. We waited for the next victim to enter and locked the door behind them.

When we were really bored, we ganged up on someone and dragged them in kicking and screaming. Eventually, we let them out, but sometimes we'd get a rush of customers, forget about them and unintentionally leave them in there too long. I confess that most times it was intentional.

The victim would scream, "It's freezing in here!" So we barely opened the door, threw in a Baskin-Robbins windbreaker, locked it again and turned off the lights. It happened so often we eventually left a chair in the freezer. To this day, I cannot go into a walk-in freezer without having a panic attack.

On the 4th of July, we expected a large crowd and therefore overstaffed. When nobody showed up, everyone left except for Alison and me. Thirty minutes from closing the fireworks ended, the movie let out next door and everybody came in for ice cream. We had half of New Braunfels packed like sardines inside our 12 x 20 store. The rest lined up in the parking lot waiting their turn. There were so many, we ran out of numbers to pull.

And they didn't just order one scoop of ice cream. No, they wanted sundaes, shakes, parfaits--any labor intensive concoction. One group wanted me to make them a whole Grasshopper Pie from scratch.

I looked at the crowd, shot the customer a dirty look and said, "Really?"

"Never mind," they said. "Just make that one scoop of mint chocolate chip each."

I thought, "Why can't you people be at home, like every other American, making homemade ice cream?"

Alison and I were all alone and overwhelmed, but we kept on serving. I was on something like my 13th Matterhorn: 7 scoops of ice cream with 3 hot toppings, whipped cream, nuts and cherries on top.

Then I turned to hand it to the customer and Alison walked right into the ice cream mountain. The store went silent and everyone stood waiting for her reaction.

With the front of her uniform covered in Matterhorn, she and I looked at each other, burst out laughing, shrugged our shoulders, and yelled, "Next."

The crowd cheered at our perseverance and we went on to serve the next 9,000 people waiting.

Keeping a sense of humor saved our sanity and kept us going through that summer. Although two of us came close to quitting, we pushed through that busy 4th of July and gained valuable self-confidence because of it.

Sure, it was just ice cream, but those 31 flavors taught us narcissistic teenagers how to be a part of something bigger than ourselves. We ran a store. We operated a business. We counted on each other. We put ourselves on a schedule and kept our commitments.

We only worked together for eight weeks at Baskin-Robbins, but our camaraderie made us lifetime friends. We learned to work together and persevere as a team. We also learned about friendships built on loyalty, trust, and walk-in freezer jokes.

My biggest takeaway from this job was when life gets hard and overwhelming; take it one scoop at a time. And if you end up with a mess, (like ice cream on your shirt), just say "Next" and move on.

My job as Ice Cream Queen helped get me

to the place I was meant to be: living a thriving life.

And if I can handle life with humor and persevere, so can you.

*A sense of humor
will save your sanity.*

~ Donna Fuller

CAFÉ COMEDIAN

My junior year of high school, I took my first public speaking class and I was hooked. In other classes, I did the bare minimum to keep just above average grades and my parents off my back. I often heard, "if you just applied yourself", but I was more interested in the social aspect of high school.

Speech class was different. I never applied myself more in all my life. I finished every homework assignment and attended every class. I even studied for tests!

I found I had a natural ability to memorize easily and to present serious topics with a humorous spin. Watergate was way more interesting when I threw in some funny.

I learned how to inform, inspire and persuade my audience. My self-esteem soared. I felt confident. I felt empowered. It was exhilarating to be up in front of people, taking command of the room and making them laugh. I loved going to class every single day because my passion had been ignited.

Unfortunately, for many years after high school, I made choices in life that left me anything but exhilarated. I focused on other people and things rather than realizing my passion. When a draining job and relationship ended, I was ready for a fresh start.

That's when I ran across an ad in the paper for a waitress job at a popular seafood restaurant. In the interview, the manager asked if I had waitress experience. I naively told him, "Besides selling vegetables, my own babysitting business, scooping ice cream, selling jewelry and cleaning teeth, this would be my first time waiting on others."

He laughed and hired me on the spot.

The café, once an old cotton gin, general store, and dancehall, now served platters of fried catfish, oysters and surf-n-turf. Their mountain of onion rings was famous and their jalapeno hush puppies were to die for.

The wait on a Friday and Saturday night was

usually over an hour. But, as long as people sat at the saloon-style bar and nursed their Shiner Bock from the tap, they were happy. Customers loved the atmosphere; old tin building, screened front porch doors and uneven hardwood floors. After tripping over them all the time, I never could figure out how anyone ever danced in there.

Every day, lunch and dinner were insanely busy and we herded customers in and out like cattle. Our sections only had five tables and sometimes that was too much to handle.

I realized the better I looked the better I felt and the bigger the tips. So I dropped my ex-boyfriend weight. I also realized the better I took care of customers the better I felt and the bigger the tips. So I took care of them like nobody's business.

My job was not only to think ahead of customers but *for* them. In most cases, I met their dining needs before they asked. And if they needed to ask for something, they never had to ask twice.

I used my old babysitting skills and impressed parents with my attention to their children's needs. Those kids had colors and coloring books in front of them and saltine crackers to snack on as soon as they sat down.

If the adult plates were delayed, I made sure the kids had their food first. That way nobody would have to listen to hungry, whiny children.

One of my most successful "upselling" techniques was telling the table about dessert first, especially within earshot of the kids. I sold more al-a-mode than any other waitress.

Their tea glasses stayed full, their beer arrived ice cold and their food piping hot. I did everything except cut up their meat for them. Those parents came to enjoy a good meal and, by God, that's what I served.

I loved the fast pace and how time flew by. I loved the instant cash and the mother lode that was rolling in! I loved serving customers and cutting up with them.

Just like in my speech class, I used the menu specials as my presentation, and every 45 minutes when the tables turned, I had a new audience. I was the Carol Burnett of the Clear Springs Café!

I felt competent and empowered. The exhilaration high was back and I loved going to work every single day.

Honestly, there were only a couple of things I didn't like about the job. I didn't like mopping floors (I don't even like to clean my own house, much less anybody else's).

CAFÉ COMEDIAN

And, I didn't like working the party room. I looked forward to working in the party room as much as I did jury duty. Tips usually went one of two ways, okay or exceptionally bad. Parties were extra-large and hard to manage. Throw in a lot of alcohol and the chances of getting a good tip were fat and slim. FYI: Drunks don't tip well.

One Saturday night it was my turn in the party room rotation and a few large groups came in who were manageable. By the feel of the money wad in my apron, I thought I'd done okay.

Relieved that I had survived the night, I felt confident no one else was coming in so I began refilling the sugar, salt and pepper shakers. After I swept the floor, the hostess came to warn me she had just seated 35 people in the party room. I groaned but headed in ready to serve, hoping it would be an easy group.

My large party of thirty-five turned out to be a bunch of wired, jabbering middle school church campers. Five weary-looking chaperones dragged behind them.

I thought to myself, "MIDDLE SCHOOLERS! Worst possible hecklers."

FYI: Drunks and kids don't tip well.

The chaperones saw my obvious look of dread and assured me, "We'll be out of your hair as soon as possible."

And then, I stopped a moment - I thought they are here to enjoy a good meal and, by God, that's what I'm serving. I cared for them like nobody's business. My babysitting and presentation skills kicked in. I took command of that room and I heckled them before they could heckle me.

First, I informed them about the dessert list, which motivated them to "save room". I persuaded them to keep things simple. Pick one: kid's fish or kid's chicken. They each got funny nicknames and amazingly enough we kept the laughter from all the heckling down to a dull roar. (If there are any mom's, teachers, and school bus drivers reading this-can I get an AMEN!).

By dessert, all thirty-six of us were good friends. On their way out each chaperone shook my hand and thanked me again and again for a much needed night off. They almost shook my arm off.

The kids said their goodbyes; I even got a few hugs. I went to clean the tables and to my surprise each kid had left me a dollar tip. But more priceless were the two dozen napkins

CAFÉ COMEDIAN

with handwritten thank-you notes spread across the long picnic table.

"It was great!"

"You were the best!"

All notes included x's and o's.

That night I learned attitude is *everything*.

The right attitude makes all the difference in the world. The right attitude has the power to change direction and outcomes. The right attitude has the power to change everything in life for the better. A bad attitude has the same power to turn everything sour.

My attitude is always up to me. At that moment, I chose to straighten up my act. I chose to offer them great service and to have fun. I chose to take care of those little hecklers like nobody's business.

Choosing the right attitude turned what could have been a night I struggled to forget into a night I will always remember.

Come on! Who gets accolades from 30 middle schoolers? That's got to be some kind of record.

My time at the Clear Springs Café taught me that I shined when I felt naturally suited for the job. I was encouraged to use my talents and skills or starve to death. The more I used them the stronger they got and the more confident and empowered I felt. The job was a great fit because I was in my element -- fun and fast paced. Kind of like me.

I knew I was in the right place to ignite my passions in my speaking class. And I knew I was in the right place to ignite my passions in my waitress job.

Funny how my speech class prepared me to wait tables and my job as a waitress helped get me to the place I was meant to be: living a thriving life.

And if I can change my attitude, so can you.

THE DATING CAFÉ

I was an exceptional waitress in my hometown, so I knew I could be one in the big city. Never in a million years did I think I could be fired for refusing to wear more makeup.

Of course, in my exit interview, which lasted a whopping 30 seconds, they refused to look me in the eye and spouted off reasons like "defiant personality", "refusal to comply", and "poor service".

Poor service! Hey, I've got 30 middle-schoolers that'll beg to differ.

And then they instructed me to "sign here" and shoved me out the door. Their only truthful complaint with me was my refusal to wear more makeup. Oh, and I wouldn't "date" customers.

Most companies discourage fraternizing with patrons. Most companies feel this might jeopardize their business. Not this place. It was highly encouraged. Rumor had it, the owners, a husband and wife team, met at her massage parlor and she carried over some of her successful business practices to their restaurant.

Most of the waitresses were former cheerleaders, members of drill teams and athletes. Looking hot was a requirement.

I have no idea how I made the cut.

To keep our girlish figures we weren't allowed to eat anything besides lemons (a natural diuretic), diet coke (which had enough caffeine to kill a horse) and saltine crackers (to sop up the other two food groups so we could finish our shift).

It was an anorexic's dream job.

Our uniforms were short-short khaki shorts and pressed white t-shirts with sleeves rolled up like James Dean. After running up and down patio stairs all day you tend to work up a sweat, which made our t-shirts wet and see through.

Business went *way* up on a really hot day.

We even had our own weight training program. Food was served on oval porcelain dinner plates and we piled them high on top of heavy duty oval trays. Everything weighed a ton so our bicep and hamstring muscles were massive from all the lifting.

The café overlooked Lake Austin and most of the regular customers were rich businessmen. In fact, the restaurant's tagline was infamous: *You come here for the view, and oh look, there's a lake too!*

We were the Hooters of our day.

I was this pretty, yet naïve, new-to-the-big-city girl, just trying to pay my rent. But still, I thought it a bit odd that our morning meetings didn't focus on the menu specials. Instead, they taught us how to apply makeup and how to properly exercise our legs, and to do Kegels to keep things firm.

I asked, "What does that have to do with waiting tables?" They said it was all part of their customer service training program. And that we should always give the customers what they wanted, no matter what the request.

At first, I thought they were talking about giving away an extra helping of beans, but I soon realized they wanted us to give away something else.

Before each shift, the owner stood in the doorway, checking to see if we complied with the dress code. She checked our mascara and foundation. She looked us over from back to front and then either gave her stamp of approval or disapproval.

I usually got the latter.

She walked around the room, clapping her hands, ordering "Makeup ladies, more makeup!"

My daily exercise routine consisted of walking 4 miles in the morning and again at night. I was solid muscle and felt as great as I looked, except for the pressure at work to look perfect. I felt judged and unworthy so I did what made sense to me. I upped my routine to 6 miles in the morning and again at night.

After all, my job depended on me looking perfect.

But regardless of my efforts, I got called into the manager's office where she gave me the spiel, "Your sales would be better if you just wore more make-up. We have a reputation to uphold and it's what our customers expect. As a result of your actions, I'm going to have to write you up."

Shocked, I replied, "Let me get this straight. I'm fit. I come to work. I do my job. And everybody likes me. But my job is on the line because I don't wear enough blush? Do you know how wrong that is?"

"Just try to do better," she replied sheepishly.

A few weeks later a customer asked me out. Having a boyfriend at the time, I politely declined his offer. That led to another pow-wow between the management and me.

"We really hope we don't lose a customer because of your neglect," they said, carefully. "Also, we ask, again, that you comply with our dress code."

They wrote me up, again.

Long before we parted ways, I knew that job wasn't a good fit for me. Sure, it felt great to be a part of an elite group of "hotties". I'd look in the mirror and think "Dayaaamm!", but I'd get to work an hour later and paranoia would set in. I'd ask everyone, "Does this apron make me look fat?"

I knew their expectations were absurd, yet for a time, I bought into their distorted beliefs, nearly killing myself in the process.

If they hadn't fired me, I might have ended up walking 30 miles a day!

Getting fired didn't make me a failure. I was not okay with their business philosophies. I was not okay with how they treated me. I was not okay with certain job requirements.

My refusal to comply is what kept me in integrity with myself, even if it did cost me my job.

If anything, I learned we cannot go against our own grain and to pay attention to what clearly feels like a good fit. That means being in a place that is aligned with your beliefs and values. Being in a place where you feel good about yourself. Being in a place where you respect and enjoy what you do and who you do it for.

I'll admit it took me several more positions to weed out the jobs that didn't meet that criteria. Some, I recognized the signs and got out quickly. Some took me longer. Some took me *a lot* longer.

Keep in mind, correcting course doesn't mean failure. It's just a process of recognizing if you are on the right path, recalculating if you are not and then aiming yourself in the right direction.

My job as a waitress helped get me to the place I was meant to be: living a thriving life.

And if I can recognize I'm off course, so can you.

THE AU NATURAL EXPRESS

To help people appreciate the service they receive, there are a few jobs I believe everyone should be required to do at least once in their life: waiting tables, serving in the military and throwing newspapers. Although I didn't join the military, I almost added it to my job list. Often, I wonder what my life would have been like if I had.

I began my stint throwing newspapers after a law firm did me the huge favor of letting me go. I thought throwing papers would be perfect for me because I am a morning person. I figured I'd knock it out before anyone got up and make some money a few days a week.

It didn't register that throwing papers is a

365 day a year job. And, just like the mailman, neither rain, nor snow, nor heat (yes, in Texas, it's already 95 degrees at 4 a.m.), nor gloom of night could keep us from our assigned routes. The only difference was we didn't get 147 days a year off!

They offered me a convenient route in the southwest part of Austin in back of my own neighborhood. They assured me it would only take 45 minutes to knock it out.

In their sales pitch, they failed to mention that the 45 minutes didn't include time to roll the papers. On weekdays, I had to be there by 4 a.m. to roll the papers in order to get them in the yards by 6 a.m.. On Sunday mornings, they wanted us there by 3 a.m. because the papers were much bigger.

On Sundays between Thanksgiving and Christmas, we had to be there by 2 a.m. because the papers were jam-packed with sales flyers, making them the size of hula hoops. It was like throwing a 15-pound dumbbell 167 times before dawn.

In the beginning, the weight of the papers along with the constant slinging motion caused pain to shoot through my left forearm so badly I thought I broke it. I vowed to never again think people faked tendonitis.

THE AU NATURAL EXPRESS

My first weekend landed in the middle of the holiday season. On that Sunday, my husband, Maverick, reluctantly agreed to help me roll the papers. When we got to the warehouse, the place was filled with people stumbling around like the guy on the Dunkin Donuts commercial, "It's time to make the donuts."

While we rolled, I visited with a couple of people about their families and their real jobs, but more importantly how to work smarter, not harder, at this job.

After a while I realized Mav hadn't said much. I looked over to find him in a zombie state and asked, "Are you okay?"

He never skipped a beat and said, "There's a big difference between staying out this late and getting up this early."

A guy across the table from me said, "You know, you can pay people to roll your papers." I hunted those people down and paid them for the next three months. I intended this job to be temporary, but once I got the hang of it, it was easy money so I kept on going.

I threw in a prestigious neighborhood and several of the streets ended in cul-de-sacs. Occasionally, I'd see a certain young guy out in his yard. We would exchange good mornings and I'd be on my way.

One day, circling at my usual speed of light, I saw him in the yard up against his house. It was still dark out so the only light came from his porch making it difficult to see.

I shouted my usual, "Good morning," and when I did, he stepped out from the hedges to the edge of the light. Although it was still dark, it was clear he was naked.

Shocked, I kept on driving, asking myself, "Did I just see what I think I saw?"

I didn't tell anybody because I kept second-guessing myself. I continued with my route and didn't see him for a couple weeks.

Same thing, I was flying through the cul-de-sac and I threw to his yard. This time, he had moved from hiding in the bushes to the middle of the sidewalk, giving me a much clearer view.

I raced past his house and drove like a mad woman back to the warehouse to report the problem. The warehouse was run by three over-worked and under-paid men. They'd all been up since 9 p.m. the night before and none of them seemed too concerned about my situation. In fact, they found it quite funny.

Okay, I found it a little funny too. But I pointed out to the manager laughing the hardest, "Gee, I'd hate for him to venture

THE AU NATURAL EXPRESS

'round the corner to your little girl's elementary school."

That shut 'em up.

The following morning one of the managers agreed to ride with me. But like when you take your car to the mechanic, of course, nothing happened. I didn't see the guy again so I began to relax.

Until a couple of weeks later.

Right when I entered the cul-de-sac the guy was waiting for me. He stepped out from behind a parked truck into the middle of the circle. The cul-de-sac was his stage, the street lamp was his spot light and the actor was very happy to see me.

I had begun carrying a camera but got so flustered that I forgot to use it. I drove back to the warehouse, ordered my manager, "Get in the car!" and I drove like a mad woman back to the scene. We rang his doorbell at 6 a.m., woke up his parents and my manager read him the riot act.

His mother screamed, "There's no way he could have done it! He's such a good boy! And besides, he's engaged!"

And I thought, "Red Flag! Red Flag!"

When I told the managers I was pressing charges against the guy, they told me it wasn't necessary and joked that I had probably done something to provoke him.

"Are you freaking kidding me?" I demanded and filed charges anyway. Yes, I could have chosen to ignore it, but I knew his behavior deserved action. His attorney postponed the hearing date four times, hoping I would give up. He was obviously disturbed. And I knew if I let it go, his side job would worsen.

Regardless of my manager's disapproval, I knew I had to protect other possible victims. I never wanted anyone to feel like I did: vulnerable, powerless and devalued. I knew if I didn't follow through, when he did it again, I would be responsible.

Unfortunately, this was not the first, or the last time I had crazy dealings with crazy men on a job. Now, I'll be the first to admit I had stirred up some serious crazy in my own life. It's true; I made choices that put me in questionable situations. And in doing so, I let others convince me that I deserved it, even though that is never the case. I no longer wanted to carry the shame and blame, and following through was a way to make amends to myself, for not thinking enough of me in the past.

Standing up for ourselves leaves us feeling empowered, valued and free; something we all deserve.

I never imagined a paper route would result in closure to parts of my past that haunted me for years. I had an obligation and opportunity to protect others and maybe save someone else.

My job throwing newspapers helped get me to the place I was meant to be: living a thriving life.

And if I can learn to stand up for myself, so can you.

*Stand up for yourself.
You will feel
empowered, valued, &
free.*

~ Donna Fuller

WEDDING PLANNER

Driving home, I agonized over telling Mav I got fired. Again. True, I didn't like working at the microchip lab to begin with, but it was a job. I found out later it was the company's plan all along to only use me until their supplies were restocked.

So, I was having a little come to Jesus meetin' with God, where I flat out told Him, "I am sick 'n tired of this happening. Of being in places I'm not supposed to be. I think I'm doing the right thing, but then this happens? And You sure aren't telling me any different. I'm feeling pretty alone here, so if I'm supposed to be doing this wedding stuff then I need a sign. It sounds like a great fit for me, but I mean, come on, at least put my business cards in my mail or something."

When I got home and opened my mailbox there were my business cards.

Growing up, my mom made a big deal out of birthdays and threw us parties every year. My favorite part was the planning. For weeks the anticipation and excitement builds. It was like celebrating all month long!

My mom taught me how to plan an event from top to bottom, when to send out invites, and required me to send out thank you cards 10 minutes after the event. Which was really strange, because my parents avoided parties at all costs.

At sixteen, I planned my parent's 25th wedding anniversary party with Mrs. Fischer's help. My grandparents donated to my cause and I secretly brought in my mom's maid of honor and my dad's best man. Luckily, they lived in Texas and were related.

I coordinated time and travel schedules and delegated job duties. I arranged for my brother and me to have our pictures taken professionally. And, I kept it a secret the whole time, a major accomplishment for me.

It went off without a hitch until we decorated their car. We wrote in shaving cream "Still Married" and "25 Years Strong", *on the paint itself.* Although Dad stayed up past midnight washing the car and buffing out the words, they stayed visible and required him to get a paint job.

I enjoyed making a big deal out of people's milestones.

As an adult, I became known for throwing some great shindigs, but making a career out of this, making money from doing something I enjoyed, never crossed my mind. Then my friend, Dardi, suggested that I think about party planning, for reals, therefore planting the seed. I thought, "Wouldn't that be fun to plan parties and get paid for it?"

Without even thinking, I ordered some business cards.

I had no real job to support me. I had no idea how to make this happen and knew I would either sink or swim. So I decided to swim, just like I did in the swim-a-thon and everything fell into place.

Two weeks later, to help support my non-paying planning career, I found a part-time job at a local police department. I worked behind a desk, babysitting a bunch of policemen and was bored out of my mind.

Then, I signed up with a woman who taught

people how to plan and cater special events. Turned out the events she planned were get-togethers like the inaugural ball for the President of the United States.

Planning events was my priority, not decorating cakes, but I knew cakes were kind of a big deal in the wedding business. So I thought to myself, "If you're going to learn to do it, you might as well get paid to learn-go get a job at a bakery."

And I did.

That meant two weeks after getting fired, I was throwing newspapers every morning, working part-time at the police station and at a bakery, all while taking event planning classes.

I come from a line of very talented artists, oil painters in particular. I, on the other hand, can't even draw stick people. But as fate would have it, I could decorate a cake like nobody's business.

At Baskin-Robbins I had picked up a pastry bag or two making ice cream cakes, but nothing more than the border on a Turtle or Grasshopper Pie. And as a nail tech, I learned to apply the right amount of pressure and keep a steady hand. At the bakery, I learned cake basics and other tricks of the trade.

About that same time, another cake

WEDDING PLANNER

decorator asked me to buy her out which supplied me with everything I needed for next to nothing. When I felt skilled enough in the basics, I quit the bakery and ventured out on my own. There was so much synchronicity happening that it was like being in the Twilight Zone- doodidoodoo doodidoodoo...

My marketing plan was simple. I would promote my wedding planning and cakes at a Bridal Extravaganza trade show. I knew I would pick up enough business to recoup my costs, and then some. I invested in one $30 ad in the Yellow Pages because the internet was just getting started. And just like when I sold swim pledges, I went door to door looking for gigs.

Because cakes were cheap to make, I made several samples and delivered them to businesses. I left free cake and my business cards in the teacher's lounge at the elementary school behind my house. I did the same thing at the law firm where my friends worked and at other businesses you might find a lot of women.

I knew one bite and the orders would start flying in-I mean, who doesn't like cake?

I started with five orders for kid's birthday cakes. I always made the cakes bigger than they ordered. I wanted enough left over for other parents to try when they came to pick up their kids.

That strategy worked. At each party more than half the parents wanted my number. Same thing happened at the next party.

It was just like the old Faberge Organics shampoo commercial, "And so on and so on and so on..."

Before I knew it, I was booked solid with cake orders.

Then, I dove into the wedding planning part of the business. I had done my homework and booked myself a booth at a Bridal Extravaganza show. I made sure I had plenty of business cards and I bribed my friend Sally with Michael Bolton tickets to help me.

I gave out free cake samples because I wanted people to try before they buy.

My strategy worked again. I put out a square white sheet cake with white butter cream icing and they lined up to taste-test. I also created a giant square chocolate sheet cake with a chocolate horseshoe on top. I covered it with chocolate butter cream icing with a fudge border. It was so pretty I didn't want to cut it. But, people were circling the table asking, "When are you going to cut the chocolate

WEDDING PLANNER

one?"

I cut the cake and it was gone in ten minutes.

I ran out of cake and business cards, but my calendar was booked solid. Eventually, I grew tired of fighting Bridezillas and cake meltdowns in the Texas heat, so I looked for a new direction. But for five years, I enjoyed making a big deal out of people's milestones.

I hadn't known my next move or how to make it happen. And I certainly didn't know I could do something I enjoyed and could get paid for it!

I look back at the microchip lab and see God did me a favor. Ironically, I was fired from a job I didn't even like! It wasn't my passion in the first place.

I was mad because I didn't think I was getting any signs, but it turned out getting fired *was* the sign. Without it, I might have never realized what I was capable of doing on my own.

Which is proof to me that man's rejection, truly is God's protection.

When I put my time, energy and talents toward something I enjoyed, others were served well because of it. Everyone benefited, including me. And with faith and footwork things unfolded quite nicely.

My job as a wedding planner helped get me to the place I was meant to be: living a thriving life.

And if I can do something that's a good fit for me and get paid for it, so can you.

WHACK-A-MOLE MACHINE

I was still doing weddings and cake orders and throwing newspapers. In addition, I was unofficially working full-time for the city with no benefits. So, I did what any other normal person would do and decided to do a job search for a *real job* that offered more security and benefits.

The next day, I ran across an ad in the newspaper for a receptionist at a civil engineering and surveying firm. All the men in my family were either civil engineers or surveyors or both. My family had difficulty grasping the whole self-employment concept, even if I was up to my eyeballs in cake orders.

Engineering, however, they could

understand. So I thought to myself, "Won't *they* be happy if I get this job?" Yep, this was a good fit, alright. For them.

It never once occurred to me that I might want to continue doing something that pleased or suited me. During my meeting with the office manager, I learned that the boring duties, pay and 3-minute drive from my house would be the same as I had in my job with the city.

I thought how pleased everyone would be if I had official, full-time job security. At this point, I had learned the definition of insanity from 12-step recovery and how well I applied it to every single one of my personal relationships. However, when it came to picking jobs, my picker was still broken. I couldn't see my pattern of repeating the same job, different place equaled the same results-- bored out of my mind and unhappy.

The office manager wanted to hire me on the spot, but she had a couple of other people she wanted to interview.

I felt faithful and fearless after submerging myself in recovery for the past two years. Although I wanted the position, I knew I had always been taken care of before and it wasn't going to make or break me if I didn't get the job.

I didn't feel like I had anything to lose, so I said, "How about I work for you part time for two weeks to see if I like it? I'm tired of getting into places that are not a good fit. If it doesn't work out for either of us then we'll part ways, no hard feelings."

"And, I'd like a dollar more per hour so I can pay for health insurance," I added.

My brain screamed, "ARE YOU CRAZY? YOU CAN'T SAY THAT TO HER!" But I stayed quiet and held my breath.

She agreed immediately.

I drove back to the city and, for the first time in my life, gave my two weeks' notice. I was antsy to get on with my new full-time position, but stayed until the end. I was proud of myself for finishing the job and I left the city feeling like a grown up.

Then I headed straight over to meet with the office manager at the engineering firm, hoping she'd offer me a permanent home; especially now that I was out of a job.

When I walked in she said, "We want you." My last day with the city became my first official day with the engineering firm.

I couldn't wait to tell my family the good news. They'd be so happy!

The firm was run by a bunch of highly educated good ol' boys and I laughed every day for the next four years. I had more fun at this job. It was one of the best places to work.

Most of the employees, contractors, and clients were University of Texas Longhorn fanatics. This was another huge score with my family because we bled orange. Growing up, our door chimes played the Eyes of Texas. In place of our family photo, we hung an almost life-size picture of Bevo and the tower over the TV. And when you opened our front door burnt orange glowed from our entry way out across the front lawn.

When football season kicked into high gear, so did the rivalry between the UT and Texas A&M fans. Lisa, a project manager, was a Texas Aggie.

That Thanksgiving weekend, the Longhorns beat the Aggies. Lisa said she'd mentally prepared herself for the ribbings she knew she was in for after the holiday weekend. However, she wasn't prepared for her office wall to be painted burnt orange from floor to ceiling, with a five-foot wide longhorn outlined in the middle of it.

Although my job duties were basic, the phone lines rang off the wall, making the hours fly by. I earned my keep by managing the incoming calls and visitors like Nurse Ratched. Nobody got past this gatekeeper without an appointment or a blood sample.

One morning, it sleeted, and then snowed, but like the mailman, I had to deliver newspapers. When I got to the engineering firm, nobody else showed up.

The phone finally rang, I picked it up and my boss said, "I knew *you'd* be there."

I felt true respect from my boss, but more importantly, from myself. I had behaved like a responsible, trustworthy employee. I felt good about me and I beamed with pride for the good job I was doing for them.

We became like a family, protective of and picking on one another. And when I shot my first deer from 200 yards away, Mav, my dad, and my guys beamed with pride for me.

It was clear I'd made the cut and from that moment on, they treated me like one of the boys.

I heard rumors that the woman handling the construction contracts was falling down on the job. Faithful and fearless again, I went to the office manager and said, "I sense you are unhappy with her performance. I don't want to know details. I just want you to know if the position becomes available, I would like a shot at the job."

Three days later they promoted me to Contracts Administrator. Now, I handled the crazy phones *and* the contracts--really, a two person job. But at least I had a job title besides receptionist. I couldn't wait to tell my family!

I worked surrounded by educated, successful people. I saw their diplomas and all their "toys" which implied they were doing well.

I had a few college hours under my belt but, due to my short attention span, I never finished. Still, I saw what my colleagues had and what they were able to afford, so I decided, again, to give college the ol' college try.

However, once I'd made up my mind to go back, I was also ready to be done, now.

I thought to move things along, why not just sign up for twelve hours? You know, on top of cakes, my full-time job and throwing newspapers. A friend said I was insane and suggested I start slow. Slow? I had two speeds: 90-to-nothing and sleep.

I decided my friend had a point and signed up for six hours at the community college. I thought I'd pick classes I liked, so I took

WHACK-A-MOLE MACHINE

Business 101 and English II. My first semester, I got all A's.

Even though my plate was overloaded, soon, I was bored sitting behind yet another desk. So I did what any other insane person would do and added more--more school hours at two different colleges in opposite directions.

After a slight nervous breakdown, I finally realized something had to give. I quit the newspaper delivery biz, only to substitute it with a significant amount of drinking, eating, and spending.

Like a whack-a-mole machine, as soon as I pounded one obsession down, three more came popping up.

And, of course, my performance at work diminished along with my boss' respect.

I decided more change would help. I came up with the bright idea that we should sell our home and move to the country. And, if that wasn't enough, I piled on yet another part-time waitress job.

I was caught up a belief system that says, "Don't just sit there DO something!" I was racing through life and from myself. I was afraid if I sat still long enough, I might figure out that there was something I was meant to do—something that would set my heart on fire.

And that was scary.

I hadn't learned that a desk job was not a good fit for me. I hadn't learned that I stayed insanely busy to feel productive and like I was contributing. I hadn't learned that piling my plate too high and then complaining about all I *had* to do, was a way for me to feel like a martyr, and that I came across like one. I hadn't learned about work life balance and that it was okay to sit still and do nothing.

I hadn't learned that I was a people pleaser and that *my* desires should come first. Shoot, I hadn't learned what my desires were.

I did learn how good it felt when people appreciated and respected me, how bad it felt when I lost their trust and how good it felt when I gained it all back.

I learned it is important to work in a fun atmosphere because time flies when you are laughing all day. My slight nervous breakdown might not have been so slight if it hadn't been for the humor. I have fond memories of my job because we laughed every day for four years.

This job taught me that because I enjoyed where I worked, I wanted to stay. I stayed happier and longer at this job than I ever had before.

It's been well over a decade since I left the firm, but many of us continue to celebrate; graduations, marriages, births, retirements and UT wins. We also came together to celebrate the life and grieve the loss, of our good friend, Tommy Dodd.

Up to this point, I considered most of my jobs, just a job. So when I moved on to my next adventure, I was surprised at how I grieved leaving the laughter. The difference that handling life with humor can make was a huge revelation for me.

I'd never thought that my job as contracts administrator would later influence my decision to do comedy, and helped get me to the place I was meant to be: living a thriving life.

And if I can recognize the importance of enjoying my workplace, so can you.

Time flies when you are laughing all day.

~ Donna Fuller

GOAT FARMER

It had gotten to the point that we were so unhappy in Austin, that I couldn't even get Mav to mow the lawn. He and I didn't see eye to eye on many things, but we did both dream of a 1,000-acre spread and a country life.

My dream included being away from the hustle and bustle of the big city and living off the land. I wanted to raise livestock and live where our pets could roam. And not be able to mouth *I need a cup of sugar* to our nearest neighbor from our own kitchen window.

Mav's dream was simple. He wanted to pee off the back porch.

"But I don't understand?" I said.

"And you don't have to" he replied.

I decided to make the dream of owning our own land in the country come true. I like to fly by the seat of my pants, so once I decided to make this happen, I had our house sold in 10 days, leaving us without a home for the next six months. We had no Plan B, but plenty of stress.

We came close to buying 23 acres, but after several failed attempts with financing, it seemed too much like work. Fearful of the unknown and of being disappointed, I kept trying to force it to happen. I would not let that property go, even though I knew in my heart it wasn't in our best interest.

Mav felt it too; at least he was brave enough to say it out loud. We decided to quit while we were ahead. Although scared and still homeless, we felt relief. As soon as I loosened my death grip and let go, I was able to hear my gut say, you're not going to believe what God has in store for you.

A week to the day later, we found our Green Acres.

Mav drove me out to the property for the final approval, assuring me this was our place to be. We drove for so long, when we arrived, I was still experiencing jet lag. All I saw was never-ending thicket and a dozer-created path that jarred our insides out.

I whined, "What happened to our wide open spaces? This is what you call Green Acres? Are you out of your mind?"

I was ready to hightail it and run. But being a surveyor, Mav had the gift to visualize the property's potential. Reluctantly, I trusted his judgment and agreed this would be our new home in the country.

Soon, we'd be living our dream, away from the hustle and bustle of the city, but now he'd have forty-five acres to mow. Since I'd hauled hay, picked vegetables and was a fan of country music, I felt I had earned the God-given right to claim country girl status.

I'll pee in the woods. I'd done it all my life. But, apparently I had become accustomed to and enjoyed the conveniences of electricity, indoor plumbing and a little thing called running water.

However, this was raw land. No lights, no potty, no taps, nothing. At that time, I had no idea how much time or money it takes to add those conveniences.

In my effort to live off the land, I started a garden, twice. The weeds and the critters took over before I could pick anything. Then I remembered how much I hated picking beans anyway, so I gladly paid the neighbor lady down the road for her vegetables. I learned it was a small price to pay when you don't like doing the work.

I also learned, it was quite a hike to our nearest neighbor, especially when you want to borrow a cup of sugar.

For the next two years, we worked round the clock to unveil the land. First we rented a ride-on trencher to dig a water line. What normally took half a day to dig, took sixteen hours as the machine inched its way through clay and rock.

We took turns driving the trencher and after finishing my first shift, Mav looked back down the line and said, "Why is it crooked?"

"Because I fell asleep," I said. That was also my last shift. Truth be told, I resembled Lisa Douglas from Green Acres more than I realized.

My husband, as former military, felt the need to secure the perimeter with a fence. We went from Green Acres to Fort Knox. One day while digging fence post holes, the auger bit broke off four feet in the ground. In order to get it out, they unhooked it from the tractor and slid a piece of drill stem pipe through the top end. Like pushing a merry-go-round, two grown men manually reversed that bit back up through the clay and rock. It took them four hours to go four feet back up. I've never heard so many cuss words in all my life.

You don't know what work is until you work full time at a real job during the day and then come home to work again until dark. We bought a single-wide mobile home that had once been used as a hunting cabin. Mav built a barn that was nicer than our house. We put in 11 utility poles for electricity and bought a hoss of a truck, tractor and trailer.

After working round the clock for a couple of years, we were sixty thousand dollars in debt, most of that slapped on credit cards. I thought to myself, "This sure is expensive and a lot of work", so I tried to talk Mav into moving to the beach.

He'd prefer to live *anywhere* else, but was so worn out he almost packed his bags.

Once I asked my friend, "Have you and your husband ever built a house together?"

She said, "Nope. We're still married."

Thinking back to my friend's warning, and how tired we were I wasn't sure our marriage could survive building a home together. Instead, we bought the adjoining 8 acres from our friends and moved into a "barndominium". It was official; from there on out, I would be raised in a barn.

The real fun came with raising livestock. We planned to raise cattle, but the college professor in my Animal Husbandry class, a veterinarian, raised goats. He taught us about breeds, sheep and goat wire and the high cost of raising cattle versus goats. Since we'd spent so much money getting our place up and running, I convinced Mav to switch over to goats.

I learned a lot in that class, but Dr. Abel's most memorable words were, "No real man can resist the sight of a baby goat."

Oh how right he was.

Raymond and Lucy were our brother and sister starter set, boar goats with chocolate heads and white bodies. Raymond was fixed, and since he was forced to give up one pleasure, he traded it for another, causing to him weigh in at 198 pounds. This was fine until he snuck into our house, where we found Raymond sleeping on the floor. You try getting a 200-pound goat out of your bedroom.

We continued collecting and our herd grew from 2 to 15, which was still manageable. However, we learned goats were part bunny rabbit. The first spring we had 19 babies in 11 days and this country girl realized I don't know nothin' about birthin' no goats!

The births came as a surprise, because Curly, the daddy, was only 5 months old. We thought it was too early to have "the talk" with him just yet. But apparently, 5-months made him a horny teenager in goat years. I can tell you one thing, if Curly had been in a sports bar he'd have been passing out cigars and getting all kinds of high-fives.

For 11 days straight, we became new parents and were a nervous wreck. We treated them like we would our own children, naming them after close family and friends and sent out emails with pictures announcing each new arrival.

We raced home after work to enjoy our babies. We loved watching them jump sideways like little skateboarders and as they played King of the Hill on anything that put any kind of height underneath them; stairs, hay bales, and fallen trees. Mav decided that wasn't good enough for his babies, so he drew up blueprint plans in AutoCAD to build them a jungle gym. That's where I drew the line.

Only a few babies needed special attention, but I loved to see them come running when it was bottle feeding time. We found it easier to bring them in the house since it took longer to walk to the barn than it did for them to down the formula. Once, our neighbor kids came over, but when they started acting up, I sent then inside, ordering them, "Go sit on the couch."

After a few minutes, I heard them running from one end of the house to the other, so I threw open the back door, hoping to catch them in the act. The children were sitting quietly on the couch as instructed, however a small herd of bottle-fed goats were running wild, playing King of the Hill on my end and coffee tables. That's when we decided it was time to feed them outside again.

Normal farmers treat their livestock like livestock, but our goats became family and our herd was now at 50. Everyone was growing up so fast, especially the little boys. Since we were trying to make money, we were forced to make the difficult decision to downsize before those little boys super-sized our herd.

When we sold all the little boys to my Hispanic friend, I knew I'd sealed their fate. Feeling like such a horrible mother, I cried a week before and a week after. At that point our goat operation turned into a retirement home after painfully realizing that although we considered them family, others considered them supper.

We still consider cabrito a four letter word and we spell it out within earshot of our goats.

I went into this with big dreams, and no vision, making everything up as I went along. Not something I suggest to anyone, even though it gave us plenty of opportunity for growth and humor.

Don't get me wrong, big dreams are vital to our lives. They are the best place to start. My dreams put me in the right mindset. They made me feel like I had choices and could succeed. Big dreams make us not want to settle for less.

Because I dreamed big we had these amazing experiences:

While swimming laps in my pool, the neighbor's three ton bull comes over to visit and treats the pool like his own personal trough.

Normal fall and winter months include massive bonfires, cooking s'mores and vegging out to the sound of the crackling fire. One night, we had 11 bonfires lit at once. Aggies would have been impressed.

The sense of self-satisfaction from feeling completely exhausted, after cutting and stacking real firewood for our wood burning stove.

Sitting on our deck at night and looking up at my very own planetarium.

I can claim I've been "raised in a barn".

Still, creating and writing down our vision would have helped us clarify our 1,000-acre plan. It would have helped us prioritize and kept us on track. It would have eased our fear, doubt and confusion along the way. Having a clear written vision would have let us manage our big dreams, money, and stress levels better.

It was an enormous job finding and building our Green Acres, especially from the dirt up. But I wouldn't trade the work, growth or life for the world. Living in the barn, I realized just how lucky I am.

My job as a goat farmer helped get me to the place I was meant to be: out on Green Acres *and* living a thriving life!

And if I can dream big but recognize the need to create a vision, so can you.

COPY QUEEN

When the drive from living in the country to my job in the city grew into a dreaded chore, I looked for work closer to home. I applied for several desk jobs. People got so excited when they saw my resume that I got offers on the spot, sometimes over the phone, sight unseen. As much as I wanted to be closer to home, I wasn't going to desperately settle for crappy pay with no benefits. My gut said don't settle, hold out a little longer.

A couple of weeks later, I was offered a job as a copy queen at a new power plant only 6 miles from our home. As usual, the desk job would not make use of my skills and would not interest me. But, my gut said if you're going to pick the same thing again, pick this one-it is one of the best places to work. So I jumped on it.

The power plant was jointly owned by the company I worked for and their partner company. However, their cultures were polar opposites. My company treated employees as their greatest assets and supported us in every way possible. They showered us with appreciation, respect, and generous benefits. It showed me how little I had been willing to settle for in the past.

Their partner company, on the other hand, allowed management to falsify time sheets, drink vodka on the job and resolve conflicts by letting employees pull box cutters on each other, which, of course, solved everything.

They kept lazy employees decades longer than they should. And, as soon as they retired, they were rehired as contractors quicker than you could file away their exit papers.

They treated employees with the utmost disrespect, but people took it because they were desperate for their retirement packages. Despite their misery, they toughed it out until they retired or died. Everything was swept under the rug, so the only evidence of this treatment was hearsay.

COPY QUEEN

I can tell you, the company I worked for valued and respected their employees more than any employer I have ever had. This was where I learned that employees respond well when they feel appreciated. We were eager to reciprocate in kind. They weren't afraid to spread the wealth and they empowered and trusted us with few limitations. For example, we were given unlimited sick leave, although we liked coming to work so much it was rarely used.

During the construction phase, it rained 36 inches in 4 months and we thought about switching from building a plant to an ark. Morale could have taken a nose dive as we drudged through the mud. Instead, it was off the charts because we were determined to build that plant on time and under budget. We wanted to do this for the company, for all they were doing for us. Their appreciation built our loyalty.

As copy queen, I Xeroxed plans all day long. I don't know how anyone could stink at making copies, but I did. Working round the clock to get the plant up and running kept me busy, but I was bored out of my mind. I would have rather turned wrenches in the rain than do what I was doing. The only thing I enjoyed was planning our company party because I got to use my skills. That, and my Pepto Bismol pink hard hat.

When the plant started up, I was promoted to Plant Administrator, which sounds better than it was. Really, I was a glorified secretary babysitting 23 men. Another desk job, only this time I was filing all the plans I had previously copied. And I was asked to do budgets, which was interesting because I don't do math.

So, I enrolled in an accelerated college program. Not accelerated in the sense it was for the gifted and talented, but accelerated in you cram three years of college into one. I did this in addition to working 50 hours a week because I wanted to make sure I never slept.

On top of that, I picked a degree plan of no interest to me because it had the least amount of math and science. The only thing I liked about college was my speech class and when I was done. I felt overwhelmed, had no passion and barely scraped by in all my classes.

I felt guilty and miserable about doing a crappy job at everything. It ate at me, so I ate to squash my feelings of guilt, misery, and boredom.

I packed on 60 pounds and then my other favorite habit kicked in. I spent every dime I made. I grasped for some way to feel better about my life and myself. Unfortunately, the more I spent, the more I ate, and the more I ate, the more I spent and I continued to spiral into despair.

And just for spice, we took in our 10-year-old nephew for a few months. Even though it was our choice, it just about put me over the edge.

For at least a decade, I had been going ninety-to-nothing. I felt burned-out and depleted. I was a pill to live with and a pill to work with. Everyone was in my line of fire, me included.

After I graduated, they offered me a business manager position, which surprised me, based on my less than stellar performance. But for once in my life, I said no. I had no interest in accounting, because again, I don't do math. I couldn't tell you what I really wanted to do yet, but I was sure that wasn't it.

Life at the plant finally settled down and we began a normal work week schedule. However, my job became even duller. The only break in the monotony was when I had to miss work to have my hysterectomy. The morning after my operation, the men from work kindly called to check on me and to ask how it felt to be field dressed.

Then on the morning of 9/11, I walked through the control room and saw the operators glued to the TV. I looked over just in time to watch the plane plow into the side of the second tower.

Downtown Houston was the hub for many energy companies, our company included. Fearful that terrorist would next target all energy companies, Houston employees were ordered to evacuate to our power plant. By three that afternoon over fifty people had escaped the potential threat and relocated to our plant. My wedding planner skills kicked in and I arranged their room and board and helped connect new emergency utilities for everyone.

When things got up and running our lunch room looked like a mini-version of the stock market floor. It felt great to use those skills and to have purpose, even if only for a short time. We all worked round-the-clock to support our team while we all grieved for our nation's enormous loss.

Next, Enron crashed in scandal and our company suffered from guilt by association. Soon after, the first of our steam turbines broke down. A month later the second turbine went off line too. We worked tirelessly for six months to get the turbines back up and running.

When the twin towers, Enron and our turbines collapsed, the confidence of our stock holders did too. Our stock plummeted. Morale soon followed, so our company's owners made cross country trips to spend one-on-one time with employees.

Hoping to boost sinking morale, they maintained we were their greatest assets and promised they would do whatever possible to get things back on track. We felt as much empathy for the company's owners, as the owners did for us. They kept their word, morale increased and things got better.

However, our partner company made us a cash deal for their share of the plant, an offer the owners could not refuse. A week before Christmas my company announced their decision to sell their share of the plant. We were given three weeks to make a decision. We could stay with our company or go work for our partner company.

For those who stayed with our company, it meant relocation and a guaranteed position, even if they had to make one up. And for those who chose not to move, they would get a job with the partner company with lifetime benefits and job security negotiated on our behalf.

I lived in a small town so if you didn't work for the energy, electric or water companies, the pickings were slim. When I shared my job dilemma and decision with my family and friends, they thought it was a no brainer. They all said, "Of course you'll go work for them. They are the best employer in the area." And my response was always, "That's because they're the *only* employer in the area."

My gut screamed NOOOO! but I did not trust it. In the end my reasons for staying were Mav, my farm and my critters. However, I allowed peer pressure and fear to drive my decision to sign those papers. And when I did, I felt like I had just come over to the dark side.

I had been treated very well by our old company and hung on to that job because of the respect and benefits, even though I wasn't interested in what I was doing. I did the best job I could and whenever I had a chance to use my skills I was engaged and passionate. But I learned if you don't have passion for what you do, no matter how good the company, it still doesn't make it a good fit.

My job as Copy Queen helped get me to the

place I was meant to be: living a thriving life.

And if I can see the positive effects that respect and appreciation have on others, so can you.

Appreciation builds loyalty.

~ Donna Fuller

SECURITY ZONE

My paycheck was coming from a different company but, I was still working at the same desk, at the same job, doing the same ol' thing. I didn't realize it yet, but I was grieving over leaving my former company. I felt I had no choice, passion or purpose.

In my sadness, I slapped over $10,000 on a single credit card, in just 3 weeks. Now I'd spent a lot of money in my time, but never before at warp speed. My spending was out of control and I saw no way out of the mountain of debt.

Tension and hostility at work grew. The difference in management styles was unpleasant. We begged our old company to take us back. They were still recovering from financial difficulties and currently downsizing. It was clear that ship had sailed.

In my misery, I looked for a change in career. My crazy mind told me, "Go back to school and get your teaching certification. Oh, and while you're at it, go ahead and sell Adirondack chairs and wait more tables!" I took my own career advice, which as usual, was adding more jobs.

My dread and depression should have been a big red flag. Every day I wrote in my journal how much I hated going to work. Depression made it almost impossible to drag myself out of bed and I'd cry myself to sleep. Or, I'd pass out from drinking gallon jugs of White Zinfandel.

And then one of my co-workers, Bill, who had also chosen to stay and my favorite high school teacher, Mrs. Kingsbury, both found out they had cancer. They died a few months after being diagnosed. Shocked and devastated by the loss, I sometimes secretly hoped that I would be next.

Still, I stayed. This made me question myself, because I'd walked out on other jobs over something as trivial as the wrong kind of toilet paper. "No Charmin! That's it, I'm outta here."

This job had me by the throat and I couldn't figure out why I felt so obligated to stay.

About that time, I found a 12-step money program to help me with my spending problem. I dug into the how, what and why of my insane money behavior. I got clear about my income and outgo. Conscious spending, saving and self-care became the foundation of my new lifestyle.

During my step work, I talked about my unhappiness at my job and a friend asked, "What do you like to do?"

I responded profoundly, "I dunno."

She said, "There's got to be something."

After hemming and hawing around for a while I said, "I like to write; I guess."

Excited at my revelation, she said, "Great! What do you like to write?"

"Um, emails", I replied. At that point, that's as much as I could share. I had no confidence, no passion, nothing.

When I was young and fearless, I just did what mattered to me. I did what I enjoyed. I didn't think it to death. But, I found as I got older, passion took a backseat to obligations.

Obligations like putting other people's happiness and needs before my own. I made choices that were a lousy fit for me because I wanted my mom and dad to be happy.

And I lived by the motto so many of us know and believe: You gotta do what you gotta do. And then, suffer through.

But, the more I learned about myself and the more I took care of myself, the more I wanted what mattered to me.

Then someone told me about a local Toastmasters club. After only one meeting, I felt a glimmer of hope. My passion for speaking was revived.

But at work, I continued in limbo, asking myself, should I stay or should I go? The more I tried to push those feelings deep down inside, the more miserable and depressed I became.

I needed an objective perspective on my situation and decided a therapist could help.

"You're just so sad," she said fighting back tears.

I thought, "Wow, I made a psychiatrist cry. I am a basket case!"

I told her, "Every day for 913 days, I've written in my journal how much I dread going to work. I'm confused, angry, miserable and depressed. I'm sixty-plus pounds over-weight and I cry every-single-day. I don't want to stay,

SECURITY ZONE

but I can't seem to go."

I continued, "People tell me all the time they'd give their right arm for my job so I try to convince myself to stay. They remind me I'll never have an opportunity like this again. It's complete job security with a pension. All you have to do is suit up and show up for the next 15 years. And you don't even have to do a very good job. This makes me believe this job is not only the key to my retirement, but my overall happiness."

She said, "Maybe, but at what price? What do you like to do?"

I said, "And there lies the problem. I dunno. I hate what I do so, of course, I'm lousy at it, but it's all I know. I am stuck in comfortable misery. I don't have any other skills, at least nothing anyone would pay me for. My head says I have no other choice."

She said, "I bet you have many skills and I think you are selling yourself short. It's just a process of figuring them out. And I think you may have a chemical imbalance. I'd like to put you on some anti-depressants to level you out."

"Can I drink alcohol?" I asked.

She paused, "Uh, no. Combining the two defeats the purpose."

"I know," I said. "I'm embarrassed that I

even asked that. But liquid courage seems to be the only kind I've got these days."

After she got me started on the drugs, I quit drinking and the haze began to clear. I decided I owed it to myself, and others, to figure out what set my heart on fire. I wasn't sure of my next move, but I knew the longer I stayed at that job, the longer I would stay.

My gut told me I had bigger, better choices, so I listened and gave notice.

At my going away party, my co-workers all signed my Pepto Bismol pink hard hat. Then they asked, "Do you think you'll wake up next week and say what have I done?"

"Not in a million years," I said, without skipping a beat.

I had limited my life by believing I had no choices. I practically destroyed myself to realize that I needed a job that fulfilled and replenished me. I learned dying a slow and agonizing death for the sake of job security was not a good tradeoff. I learned to trust my gut.

I learned to pay attention to the signs around me and to recognize when I needed help. Because when you dread what you do and are depressed, that's a sure sign it is time to look for something that ignites your passions.

SECURITY ZONE

Leaving my job was my turning point and helped get me to the place I was meant to be: living a thriving life.

And if I can trust my gut enough to go discover what sets my heart on fire, so can you.

*The best therapists
have four legs
and the ability
to save your sanity*

~ Somebody really smart

RESCUE MOM

Part of any solid 1,000-acre plan includes dogs, cats and other critters running around. However, I was not raised as a pet lover. In fact, there was a time when I couldn't stand to have a cat brush up against me.

My friend, Adam, happily pointed out, "You know, there is something wrong with a person who doesn't like animals."

Although he knew me well, he had no idea.

I had attempted pet parenting only a few times. As a child, I had one dog for a little while. I also had goldfish--which I petted to death.

During a low point in my life, I got two kittens so I could have something to love.

Once, I threw clothes into my washing machine, set it for a low load and went to work. Luckily, I left the lid open so the machine only filled a few inches with water and stopped. I came home to a screeching wet kitten trying to claw her way up the slippery agitator. She wasn't hurt, but boy was she mad. I felt like a horrible mother.

Now that we had land, it was time to start bringing pets on board, even though my previous attempts had failed. So, in my infinite wisdom, we got three puppies; back to back—no stress there.

Our first child, Buddy, was a golden lab. He wandered up to a friend's home and Jeff offered him to us. He was only four months old, but behaved like a little old man; mild mannered with a gentle nature.

If you were friendly, Buddy would force himself between your legs to get your attention and sit there until he got scratched. He welcomed and accepted everyone who came through our door, both two-legged and four-legged.

Except one time. When our plumber came out to give us an estimate Buddy greeted him. They made friends and soon he was in between the plumber's legs. But when the plumber's helper got out of the truck, Buddy came unglued. In a matter of seconds the hair on his back stood straight up, he barked and growled uncontrollably and then our gentle giant lunged toward the man as if to attack him.

By this time, Buddy was eighty pounds so it took all my strength to reel him back in. The helper quickly got back in the truck and refused to get out.

Buddy never acted like that again. Truth be told, I was a little glad to know he had it in him. We often wondered about his prior life. At first we thought he might have wandered out of his yard and gotten lost. After that reaction, we began to wonder who or what he had escaped from.

Although Buddy's large size and golden breed were considered a double whammy in the longevity department, he surprised everyone and lived to be almost fifteen.

Now, when we talk about Buddy, everyone says, "He was such a *good* dog."

People said he was lucky to have had us, but we knew it was the other way around.

I picked up Lady, our Australian cattle dog, after driving past a sign on the highway. It was spray painted on a broken piece of particle board, "Cow pups for sale", in what looked like a child's handwriting.

I thought to myself, "We'll have cows one day, we're gonna need one of those!" I whipped back around and drove down a long driveway to the back of a heavily thicketed area. I parked in front of a run-down mobile home and instantly twenty dogs surrounded my truck. They were blackish blue or red; all with freckled legs.

A man and a woman dressed in raggedy clothes came out to greet me. Unsure about the dogs and afraid of getting shot, I rolled down my window and shouted, "I'm here to see the puppies."

"It's ok," they yelled back as they waved me into their house.

Nervous, I walked across the front porch filled with gaping holes. They warned me, "Don't fall through." I swear I heard Deliverance music playing in the background.

The couple led me into the kitchen to a make-shift corral made out of connected baby gates, which held a dozen of the fluffiest blackish blue or red puppies I had ever seen; all with freckled legs.

"How much", I asked?

"Twenty bucks," she said.

"What a steal", I thought. I picked out our

new little girl and handed the woman a twenty.

Lady looked soft and fluffy on the outside, but on the inside, she was in a constant state of PMS; controlling, irritable and sometimes just plain mean. I'd have sworn Lady was me, reincarnated.

During her thirteen years, Lady tolerated me but was loyal to Mav. She would follow him everywhere he went on the tractor and she could chase a cedar stick like nobody's business.

Lexi, an eight week old, full-blooded Golden Retriever also came to us through a friend. A woman I worked with bought her for her two young daughters. When she brought her to the office I thought she was the most beautiful puppy I had ever seen.

Three months later the woman called me to say Lexi's jumping was out of control, the girls were terrified of her and that her husband had no patience for the dog.

"Do you want her?" she asked.

The next day, I rescued an attention-starved puppy from their backyard where she had been banished. She bounced for joy all the way to my truck where I put her in the back seat. I hadn't driven a block before she curled up and fell fast asleep. Her peaceful state told me she knew she was going to her forever home.

Lexi and Buddy hit it off immediately and were friends for life. Lady, on the other hand, was a stinker and should have been an only child. Somehow they worked out their differences, because all three of our puppies caused plenty of trouble.

Mav and his dad spent two weekends underneath the trailer home, laying on rock, tacking up sticky, pink insulation. But they hadn't had a chance to cover it with plastic sheeting yet. A few days later, around two in the morning, I heard Mav jumping up and down in the middle of the living room screaming NOOOOO!

"What's wrong?" I asked.

"Just listen!" he yelled.

You could hear the dogs ripping the insulation to shreds. What had taken two full weekends to install was uninstalled in 30 minutes by three mischievous puppies.

We didn't have time to clean it up before we went to work which gave them the entire day to engage in more criminal activity. Our yard looked like a cotton candy factory had exploded. And for the next year, we picked up scattered insulation across all forty-five acres.

Another time, I decided to take a nap. I

took off my wedding ring, laid it on the arm of the couch and went to sleep. After I got up, Lexi snuck inside and I didn't notice until the next afternoon that my wedding ring had gone M.I.A.

Pooped out somewhere on forty-five acres are thirteen diamonds and a golden band. But I didn't care how much it cost, I wasn't digging for it.

I liked the idea of bringing the dogs home, but I had one rule; they weren't coming in my house. So, Mav decided to build them their own houses.

Well known for his overkill tendencies, Mav came home with a stack of eight-foot sheets of one-inch oak with matching 2 x 6's, corrugated tin, a five gallon bucket of water sealant, eight cinder blocks, a roll of hunter green plush carpet and two heat lamps.

"Are you adding on a room?" I asked.

He planned for two dog houses. One would be a double wide for Buddy and Lexi to share. He would build a separate mother-in-law suite for Lady, since she liked her personal space and was such a pill to live with.

Once finished, he brought me outside for final approval. Obviously proud of his carpentry work and grinning from ear to ear he presented the Taj Mahal with wall to wall carpeting.

Amazed, I asked, "Can I move in?"

One bone-cold morning, a few months later, Mav was leaving for work. He opened the back door, stepped back and all I heard was, "Uh oh."

I met him at the back door. All that remained of the dog houses were two tin roofs lying flush on top of the cinder blocks with ashes smoldering underneath.

We looked down at Buddy staring up at us like, "Don't look at me, I didn't put the heat lamps in there."

That's when my outside rule went right out the window and the dogs came inside to live with us forever. Before I knew it, I found myself sandwiched in between two eighty-pound dogs in my bed. And I thought, "What happened to me?"

When we brought these critters home, I had no idea how they would impact my life. They were genuinely happy to see me, always wanted to touch me and I could do no wrong; even when I barked at them.

When I left my job at the power plant to discover my passions, I had no idea where that would lead. Some days I was faithful and fearless, other days I was nervous, and okay, *terrified* about my future. But, when I looked down at my office floor and saw my furry support group, I felt safe and accepted. Despite my fears, they kept me moving forward, especially when they wanted to go for a walk!

For decades, my heart was hard, but their unconditional love softened me. That softening opened me up to discover my passions - what really made my heart sing.

And spending time with them taught me huge lessons:

- ➤ Do what comes naturally
- ➤ Take care of myself
- ➤ Do what makes me happy
- ➤ Provide unconditional service to others

I believe the old saying:

Dogs have a way of finding
the people that need them
Filling an emptiness we don't
even know we have.

A couple years ago, I visited my friend Adam. When his dog jumped in my lap, knowing me, he tried to shoo him off. But I said, "It's okay," and as I loved all over him, the dog settled down and laid peacefully up against me.

Shocked, Adam looked at me and asked, "What happened to you?"

I just smiled and said, "You have no idea."

My job was to rescue them, but really, they rescued me; and helped get me to the place I was meant to be: living a thriving life.

And if I can soften, so can you.

WORDSMITHER

Leaving the power plant took a complete leap of faith, even though I wasn't sure of my next step. I had some ideas and I knew I could write. I had the gift of gab and enjoyed going to my Toastmasters meetings. I knew I wanted to do something I loved and get paid for it. I knew I needed a break and time to decompress.

And I knew I had always been taken care of and would somehow find my way.

I announced my intention to be a freelance writer. I didn't know what that meant exactly, but it sure sounded good.

My parents had always encouraged a writing career for me, so I thought they would be thrilled when I shared my new job title. However, when I told my dad I had traded job security and a pension plan for the life of a freelance writer, he turned an ugly shade of gray.

He said, "Do you know how long it takes to get published?"

I laughed and said, "I think I'll be okay."

Two weeks later, I had my first article in the Smithville Times. I only got paid $10, but I was published.

Then, the editor asked, "Do you know anything about alcoholism or debt?"

"I wrote the book," I told him, and I got those assignments.

Writing opportunities came to me from many directions. I was doing work I loved and getting paid for it. But the transition of going from a steady paycheck to a *maybe* paycheck gave me panic attacks.

To bury my fears, I ate. Usually, I'd eat when I didn't know what to type. When I was scared, which was most of the time, I'd stand in front of my fridge, doors wide open, looking for something to take the edge off.

For over twenty years, I had a system; I would lose twenty pounds, just in time for swimsuit season. I'd live on Diet Coke, maybe with soup and crackers, and walk almost 10 miles a day. Then I would gain it all back during my fall fat season; knowing I could lose it again come spring.

But as I got older, I learned that weight goes on more quickly than it comes off. I tried everything to drop the pounds. Pumped up and ready to go, I'd start on a Monday because that's a great day for a fresh start. By Friday, I was back to eating everything in sight. After a while, I couldn't even make it to Tuesday.

Weight Watchers worked well for me when it was exchanges, but when they changed to a points system, I gained weight. Of course, it was because I ate my twenty-five points in Cinnabons. Hey, they were on the list.

I tried the South Beach Diet because it had beach in the title. I dropped 30 pounds quickly, but once they gave me the green light to re-introduce carbs, the weight poured back on.

I tried Overeaters Anonymous, but when they said I could pick my own food plan, I thought, isn't that's what got me here? I tried portion control, but it seemed the more I tried to control my food, the more my weight spiraled out of control. Then, I clobbered myself, relentlessly, for not having the willpower to stay on track.

My closet looked like J.C. Penny's with

clothes in every size and color, except worn and outdated. Still, I held on to them because I might need them someday, even though I had given up on exercise and my skinny season altogether.

During the months while I was settling into my writing career, I was on an all-carb diet. I grazed through the days in a fog. I couldn't focus and I floundered. The only constants were my eating and my fear.

While my energy and enthusiasm for my work remained high, my weight gain sapped my confidence. Eventually, I stopped going to my Toastmasters meeting because I couldn't stand for anyone to see me, especially on stage.

I knew something had to change or nothing would change. But the food was my lifeline and I was scared to cut that cord.

Now they say you aren't supposed to start a diet on New Year's Day. Believe me, I had tried that before. I even paid big bucks for a gym membership, but like most people, I quit two weeks later. I loathed myself so much that I was willing to try anything. I knew change had to happen if I was to move forward. I decided to make getting this weight off once and for all my new primary job.

On New Year's Day, I drove an hour to the

church where they held the Grey Sheeters Anonymous meeting. Faithful and fearless I walked down the sidewalk. I stopped at the door and took a deep breath before I went in. The door was locked. "Are you kidding me?" I screamed towards the sky.

I sighed in relief and thought, "I tried. Guess it wasn't meant to be." This was the justification I needed to keep doing what I was doing. I told myself I would settle for a life of being fat and miserable. I returned to my car to go find something to eat.

Just as I got in my car, some meeting members drove up and gently told me, "Get to our temporary meeting NOW." I guess they thought I was going to make a run for it, so one of them invited herself to ride along with me. Before I could say no, she was in my passenger seat ordering me to *drive*.

I sat around a dining room table with a group of people who had experienced significant weight loss, but more importantly, they had managed to keep it off, some for decades. They were happy, healthy and focused. Everything they said rang true for me and I desperately wanted what they had to offer.

I was in so much pain I told them, "Just tell

me what to do and I'll do it." They shared their food plan which was simple, yet structured. I was nervous, but knew I thrived on structure and left the meeting hoping my new job would be a success.

The next three weeks were hell. I'm not going to sugar coat it. Apparently, I didn't like people telling me what to do as much as I claimed and I fought their structure like a kid fights sleep. Plus, coming down off that carb high put everyone in my line of fire. It's a period in my life I like to refer to as, thank God nobody died.

Soon, I started to level out and within six months, I lost 60 pounds. Funny though, it wasn't until I started weighing and measuring my food that I realized my portion sizes were four to five times greater than they were supposed to be. And, so was my butt.

For the first time, I had a color analysis done and I got myself measured. I can't tell you how good it felt to wear colors that looked good on me, bras that fit and to get out of those granny panties. I gave away twelve contractor bags full of outdated, worn out clothes, determined never to need them again.

I was happy and healthy. Since my head wasn't obsessed with the food in the fridge, I focused more on realizing my passions.

My Toastmasters meeting had dissolved, so I looked for another. The first group I saw was called Laughing Matters. When I read they were a humor club, I knew to look no further.

I gave frequent speeches and more writing opportunities came to me. As my writing became more consistent, it became stronger, funnier and my confidence soared. I felt creative, competent and productive.

It's been over eight years since I started my weight loss job and I've maintained it longer than any other. My food plan is structured and simple. It keeps me grounded and clear. I look forward to following this plan every day for the rest of my life. Not only did it save my life, it gave me one.

Becoming a freelance writer fed my passion and tapped into my superpowers. I applied the structure from my food plan and healthy lifestyle to working as a writer. I found the self-discipline, structure and focus inside me, necessary to succeed. And as I consistently pursued my writing, I got better at it and money-making opportunities flowed in.

With better focus came the ability to continue searching for complimentary passions. I paid attention to what made me feel alive. I persistently followed the path that felt right, refining what I wanted and what I needed along the way.

Pulling my head out of the fridge helped me deal with the fear about the maybe paycheck and the blank page.

Had I not faced my deepest fears, kept looking for a solution, and been willing to keep moving forward, I could not have succeeded as a word smither. My job helped get me to the place I was meant to be: living a thriving life.

And if I can face my fears, so can you.

THE NUTTY PROFESSOR

Through my membership in Toastmasters, I re-ignited my long dormant passion for speaking. I wanted a job where I could feed that passion. Since I had been a great babysitter, I decided I would make a great high school speech teacher. Leaving the power plant for this profession would be easy to explain and would please my mom and dad to no end.

After one semester at teacher school and observing a high school speech class, I realized I didn't like kids. Not all kids, just the ones that talked back, which was most of them. So, I stayed miserable at the plant for another couple of years.

However, after I left the plant and while trying to realize my vision as a freelance writer, I considered pursuing the teaching profession again. I thought perhaps it had seemed horrible because I had been miserable. Maybe it would be different now.

At least I had the where-with-all to think, "Before you invest the next two years in school, why don't you test the waters as a substitute teacher?"

I forgot how poorly we treated subs when I was in school. And back then, we had manners and were afraid of our parents. The administration saw me coming a mile away and signed me up as a sub before I had a chance to sit down. They asked me what grades I preferred and told them I would try any except middle school. There wasn't enough money in the world for me to teach that age group.

Guess what? I still didn't like teaching back-talking high school kids.

Second and third graders were the best. They could wipe their own behinds and, although a bunch of Chatty Cathy dolls, they didn't talk back as much.

Pre-schoolers were cute as buttons, but I couldn't just hand them a pair of scissors or a crayon and say, "Get after it." Everything I knew how to do instinctively, I had to rethink and then teach them, step by step. They wore me out and I had to go home and take a nap.

After a couple of meltdowns, I told the administration I wasn't cut out to be a teacher. The principal said, "Not everybody is, and I wish more teachers would test the waters beforehand like you."

A few months later, I took a position with Job Corps as a Career Preparation Specialist. I thought I would be the guidance counselor and loved the idea of being in a mentoring position.

By that time, I'd had enough therapy myself, and sponsored people in 12-step programs to believe I would be good. I fantasized about guiding one person at a time, especially sharing my own experience of what not to do.

After I took the job, to my dismay, I found out the students ranged in age from 16 to 24. I had jumped from the frying pan into the volcano. I figured since I despised working with regular high school students, why not teach AT-RISK teenagers, most with criminal records and unresolved abandonment and anger issues?

Yes, this will be so much better.

This job had RED FLAGS written all over

it, but I remembered my friend saying how much he loved working there. Sure, take career advice from a man who started out his day with a Big Gulp filled with Vodka.

The students lived on campus and came there to receive their GED and/or learn a trade. Some of the kids wanted to be there to create a better future for themselves.

The rest were not there by choice. The majority were either court-ordered or family-mandated to be there. They had been shipped away from everything they had come to know and love; friends, dysfunctional families and gangs.

During the six-week transition period between arriving on campus and starting their programs, they would learn basic interviewing, communication and money management skills. For eight hours a day, they were dumped in a classroom along with thirty other terrified, rebellious, angry and hormonal kids.

Not any classroom; my classroom.

I came up with a coping strategy. I used positive thinking to make the most of this opportunity. I would be in front of a live audience each day which would help me hone my speaking skills and keep me thinking on my feet. It would bring steady income, calming

THE NUTTY PROFESSOR

some of my terror. The parts I didn't plan for: Tough crowd. An uncontrollable bunch of hecklers. A comedian's worst nightmare. Anyone's worst nightmare.

The first thirty minutes of class tended to be peaceful because I had them color in coloring books like second-graders. That kept their attention. Things usually went downhill from there.

Most of them did whatever they wanted, which pushed all my control freak buttons. It was a constant struggle of wills. I screamed and yelled nonstop. Each day I got nuttier. I heard one kid tell another, "Boy, she's really trippin' today." The monster I'd become wasn't fun for any of us.

Despite their behavior, I looked at mine and decided I wanted to do better. I imagined where some kids came from and my heart ached for them. I thought to myself, what would my favorite teacher, Mrs. Kingsbury, do?

Mrs. Kingsbury had been kind, funny and fair. She was supportive and respectful. She empowered and trusted us with few limitations. I decided to be like her. I wanted to show those kids empathy and appreciation, something I knew they probably never got. I felt if I did, I might get some back. It had worked for Mrs. Kingsbury.

I picked my battles. The next day, I apologized to the class for my behavior and told them I would try to do better. Their mouths hit the floor. Then, I suggested that together we set some ground rules.

We all had limited attention spans, me included, so I agreed to teach in 45-minute intervals allowing breaks in between. I asked that they give me their full attention during teaching time and, in exchange, they could bring in snacks and drinks and listen quietly to music during breaks. I rewarded their good behavior with praise, homemade cookies, and treats.

We talked about things that interested them. As I shared my life experiences and showed them my human side, they slowly let me into their lives.

I learned that former gang members often had a teardrop tattooed at the corner of their eye. If the tear drop was clear, it meant someone close or a member of their circle (or gang) had lost their life. Colored in, meant they had killed someone themselves.

Although they mentioned it in general conversation, I knew the students told me to protect me.

There were still bad days as all of us were adjusting, but everyone lightened up and we started to get along. They began to take ownership of the rules and ordered the troublemakers to behave.

Some of the students wrote me sweet notes comparing me to Hilary Swank's character in the movie Freedom Writers. I watched the movie and realized what an enormous compliment I'd been given.

One day, we were talking about money. I shared some of my crazy behavior with money and asked them to write about their money history. I must have hit a nerve because after writing a little bit, a young girl got upset and defensive. She called the assignment stupid and refused to go on. I empathized with her pain, so I knelt down beside her desk to speak to her privately.

Before I knew it, she jumped up, threw the desk across the room and chased me down the hallway screaming, "I'm gonna kill you!" It took four male teachers to hold her back. She meant it.

The department head defended the student, telling me "she was just having a bad day." She blamed me for not following the curriculum.

When she refused to support me, I went to my classroom, packed my things and went home for good.

I cried all the way home. I felt horrible leaving those kids, but I realized, at any given moment, I could be somebody's next colored-in teardrop.

Even though it turned out to be a terrible fit, this job taught me about empathy and compassion. When people drove me nuts, I considered their background and struggles. Sometimes, it helped to picture him or her as a five-year-old, tennis shoes untied, sweet and vulnerable. In that light, I didn't take their behavior so personally.

By sharing my own background and struggles, I strengthened my connection to others. After hearing some of their stories, I stopped complaining about my childhood. Compared to them, I had it pretty darn good.

I learned to take responsibility for my own actions, no matter how anyone else behaved. And, when I did, the dynamics changed. Students trusted me more, showed me greater respect and I gladly returned the favor.

This also gave me another opportunity to stand up for myself when I wasn't supported or protected by an employer. I knew I had to

THE NUTTY PROFESSOR

leave to stay in integrity with myself.

I tested the waters instead of diving in head first. I was proud of myself for slowing down and thinking things through. And, for being more selective when it came to choosing a position that would benefit me, was a complement to my vision and would not divert me from it. Passion instead of obligation was driving my choices.

This experience reminded me that I made the right choice having four-legged kids instead of two-legged because they don't talk back and I don't have to put them through college. I was not cut out to teach the young two-legged kind again. However, teaching the four-legged kind would soon be another story.

My job as the nutty professor helped get me to the place I was meant to be: living a thriving life.

And if I can take responsibility for my actions, so can you.

*Allow passion,
not obligation,
to drive your choices.*

~ Donna Fuller

WINE AMBASSADOR

When my friend, Bill, suggested I'd make a great Wine Ambassador, I hesitated. He explained, "You'll stand there, look pretty, give away free alcohol and get paid. I mean what's not to like?"

It sounded good, but I still wasn't sure it was the right fit since White Zinfandel was no longer my friend. I wasn't worried about falling off the wagon because I enjoyed my food plan and being skinny way too much. I worried about how I was going to sell it when I could care less about it.

See, up until then, I knew my passions were speaking, writing and humor. I knew those gifts came naturally. I knew that's *how* I wanted to do things.

Apparently, I'd reached a deeper need for meaning because now it was important that I believe in the cause behind what I was doing. Living my passion was beginning to trump all other factors, except money, and I needed money.

Selling wine was a better fit for me than teacher duty. I signed up and decided to stay focused on the positive aspects of the job: I would get to perform in front of a live audience each day and it would bring steady income, calming some of my financial terror. Meanwhile, I would keep looking for the cause that would set my heart on fire.

The gigs were in grocery and liquor stores, at antique festivals and other wine-lover events. I'd haul in my equipment: rectangle card table, a half-dozen bottle openers, and one-ounce plastic cups, as required by law.

My tablecloth was black and I used a neon green Ninja Turtle Easter basket for an ice bucket. Most of the store wine stewards said it looked cool, but I used it because it was a great attention-grabber. When it grabbed a kid's attention, I grabbed the parent and offered them a wine sample, telling them they deserved it.

Some said, "No, thank you", others asked for the bottle.

Since I don't drink, the half-empty leftovers tended to stack up in my kitchen until I gave them away. After one gig, I stopped at a convenience store and offered my five bottles of leftovers to a weary-looking woman pumping gas into her beat up mini-van.

"I figured you could use it," I told her.

"You have no idea," she said, almost crying.

At the gigs, I restocked shelves, mopped floors and made sure everything was left the way I found it. I was flexible and willing to do just about anything, but I had my limits. I knew serving cheese and crackers would pair nicely, but that required me to wear a hair net and that was something I would not do.

Being a Wine Ambassador required me to engage every person who walked by and ask, "Would you like to try some wine?" Some said no, but I had to ask, so I didn't take their rejection personally.

My record in a three-hour shift for engaging customers was 387. I like to talk, but I went home that day and collapsed in a heap.

When I did gigs on an early Sunday afternoon I would see a lot of ladies dressed up in their best, fresh out of church. Many of them looked at me like I was serving grape juice straight from the devil.

Their Holier-than-Thou glare told me they thought it was a cardinal sin. A sin I obviously committed, since I was selling it.

"No. *I* don't drink," they would say, condescendingly and walk away as fast as they could.

They were flabbergasted when I shot back, "Hmm, neither do I. I just serve it, don't drink it."

Most people who wanted a sample asked, "What does it taste like?"

"You tell me," was how I normally dodged that bullet. It wasn't good for business if I told them I thought it tasted like rubbing alcohol.

If they pressed the issue, I'd say, "You know, everyone's taste buds are different. Really, only *you* can be the judge." Most nodded their heads, respectfully agreed, drank their one-ounce portion and walked away happy.

Then, there were some who insisted on my opinion. At that point, I would flip the bottle around and read the back label out loud:

"*Rich* boysenberries and *sweet* cherries. *Luscious* vanilla, *Juicy* and *silky* with lingers of black licorice. It also says you're supposed to get excitement with every sip. Is that what *you're* getting?"

In my experience, there are three categories when it comes to wine customers: true connoisseurs, wannabes and newbies who were green about the grapes.

The savvy, secure in their vino knowledge, wanted to tell me all about the grapes and regions, brag about their trips to the vineyards and claim fame from personally meeting the winemaker. I glazed over at grapes.

The wannabes swooshed the wine around like mouthwash and threw out words like, "full-bodied, robust and reserved" – like they had heard on TV.

One big shot demanded to know, "What kind of barrel do they use?"

"Um, round?" I replied.

The newbies were clueless, but at least they were up front about being wine illiterate. Well, most of them anyway.

Once, I was selling a Moscato, and a newbie started to quiz me. It was obvious he was a newbie because he couldn't even say Moscato. Then, he asked me, "What kind of grape do they use?"

"Free-range" I told him.

He said, "Uh-huh. They must come from

the Napa area."

I just knew to offer some of the newbies something sweet. If not, they'd take one sip, make a face like they just ate a pickle and look around for a place to spit it out.

Some, even if they didn't like it after a taste, slammed back the rest, telling me, "Wasting it would be alcohol abuse."

There were always people in motorized shopping carts so I would say, "I know you're driving but..." Some took me up on my offer; others waved me off, "Oh, I really shouldn't." To those I said, "I'm not gonna give you the whole bottle, just a swig. If they pull you over, it won't even register."

The sign on my table read "WE ID". I don't know who was more disappointed; the younger ones when I asked or the older ones when I didn't.

Mother's Day weekend, I made it a point to ID any women who looked over 35. They usually blushed and said, "*Really?*" Flattered, they'd pull out of their ID. I'd pretend to check it, tell them, "My gift to you," and hand them their one-ounce sample.

Being a wine ambassador turned out great for me. I enjoyed people watching and I got to visit with people from all walks of life. I found

I didn't have to drink wine to sell it.

At other jobs, when I was miserable, my work ethic was terrible. And I was consumed with guilt and shame because I wasn't raised like that. However, when I enjoyed what I was doing I turned into a workhorse and went above and beyond the call of duty.

I acted professionally and people treated me with respect and appreciation. In turn, I respected myself and my self-worth escalated.

This job let me make the most of my natural talent for performing. Being in front of a live audience kept me thinking on my feet and helped me polish my speaking skills.

The constant practice as a Wine Ambassador kept my creative juices flowing. I started winning awards for my Toastmasters speeches. It also helped strengthen my funny bone because each gig was filled with funny moments, both strange and ha-ha.

And somehow, by practicing my skills and focusing on the positive aspects of the job I was doing, I found what set my heart on fire. My passion was right in front of me the whole time, wagging its tail. It was time to speak for my pets, because, after all, they rescued me.

During my job as a Wine Ambassador, I discovered what set my heart on fire and it helped get me to the place I was meant to be: living a thriving life.

And if I can bring positive energy to whatever job I have, so can you.

DOG FOOD DEMONSTRATOR

The wine gigs were a great fit for several reasons: I enjoyed meeting and talking to people, it was fun, and I sharpened my sales and speaking skills. The company was happy that I went above and beyond for the customers and they did the same for me.

Still, I didn't feel passion about what I was doing. I wanted to work for a cause I believed in. I began taking an inventory of all my previous jobs. I looked at what worked, what hadn't and why. I looked at what I liked and disliked about each job and how my behavior either helped or hurt my position.

I made amends to every employer I'd been a pill to work for, and to those I had stolen from. I might have done it sooner, but was afraid the statute of limitations hadn't passed.

As I cleared away the wreckage of my past, the possibilities for my future looked bright. I realized pets were my passion. They had taught me valuable lessons and changed my life. Clearly, this was my cause, although I thought to myself, "Good to know, but what job should I do?"

A week later, I ran across an ad that sounded interesting:

PET LOVERS WANTED/ SALES DEMONSTRATOR

The ad read:

Premium dog food company looking for enthusiastic individuals to demonstrate and sell dog food in pet stores.

I reviewed the requirements: *Pet lover*: definitely. *Enthusiastic*: absolutely. *Sales experience*: ever since my vegetable stand. *Demonstrate dog food*: I don't have to *taste* it, do I?

Please attach resume and include some information about your pet or your experience with animals.

Oh, have I got some stories for you.

The pay wasn't great, but my gut said this

was something I could get behind. I could sell animal health. I knew I wanted the job badly, because if it had come down to it, I would have tasted the dog food.

I was still doing wine gigs, but now I found myself obsessed with scanning people's grocery baskets for pet related items, hoping to strike up a conversation about their pet food. I knew when I sold them on the pet food, but forgot to sell them wine, it was time to hang up my corkscrews.

The wine representatives tried to convince me to stay. I was tempted because of the pay, but I knew in my heart, pets were my thing. Somehow I knew it would lead to greater opportunities.

I'd haul my former wine tasting card table, along with a new royal blue tablecloth and food sample cartons into each pet store. All across Texas, I would stand there, look pretty, give away free pet food, and love on critters. I mean-what's not to like?

I was invested in my own healthy lifestyle, so I made it my mission to do the same for pets. Believe you me; in between customers I compared a bag or two of pet food. In the process, I realized my own dogs and cats were on junky food and I felt like a terrible mother.

Inevitably, they became test dummies for the good stuff.

I kept an eye on cost and portion sizes and on their skin, coat and poop. I gave customers an honest, educated opinion based on my personal experience. Unlike the wine, this was something I refused to sell if I couldn't stand behind it.

The product and its reputation were solid, so I sung praises for their pet food whenever I could. I thrived and every conversation I had, inside and outside the job, lead to the subject of animal health.

Not only did I sell food, I sold everything from beds, to harnesses, to dog bikinis. Then I learned about the importance of dog training. So, like wine and cheese, I began to pair the two.

Since I already had a connection with the customer, it was easy to convince them that good food *and* training were a must. The trainers loved me for it and they returned the favor by recommending my brand.

While serving wine I had fun conversations, but they were no comparison to the connections I made with other animal people. We shared stories about their breeds, fosters and rescues, and tears about their losses.

DOG FOOD DEMONSTRATOR

Eighty-year-old men would whip out their cell phones like gunslingers to show me their pictures of Fluffy.

The stores were filled with critters that meowed, barked and squawked. I met several unique two-legged and four-legged individuals and started collecting material for speeches.

Let me tell you about Optimus, a German shepherd puppy. While loving on him, he blew puppy breath in my face and sweetly licked my nose, so I assumed we had established a trusted relationship. Well, you know what they say about assumptions.

Optimus thought I was eyeballing his biscuit. His guard-dog instincts kicked in, he jumped in my face and bit me on the cheek. No blood, but there were teeth marks. The owner apologized profusely for his puppy's behavior and I apologized for mine.

With both my ego and cheek bruised, I returned to my table in tears.

> **LESSON LEARNED:**
> Never smooch with the pooch,
> When he's eating his grub,
> He'll think you be stealing,
> And you'll come back with a nub.

I'd made animal health my mission. I had done my homework, so I knew great pet food meant a pet could live fifteen years instead of eight. I knew a trained dog meant one less in an animal shelter.

However, I hadn't counted on being overinvested in the cause. When customers rejected my product, I felt like they were rejecting the care of their pets and I took it personally; very personally.

Eventually, I over-did my steamroller approach with a customer and got banned from a pet store. It wasn't the end of the job, but I knew I needed to re-evaluate my sales methods. I needed to balance my passion with positive energy.

As part of my honest-Abe philosophy I used the product, so I knew what a difference it made. My knowledge gained me credibility in the pet industry and added solid sales numbers to my resume.

I built my connections on trust because I stood behind the product and the cause of being a good pet parent.

Instead of putting obligation or money first, I maintained integrity with myself by trusting my gut and trying something that was a perfect match with my passions. I felt empowered.

I learned to be a better pet parent and appreciated my pets more. My on-the-job-training extended their lives by several years, a priceless bonus.

Each shift made me a stronger speaker, giving me material for speeches and a book, *Dog Food Diaries.*

God threw me a bone with this one. My work environment was filled with furry, four-legged therapists, which helped me continue to grow personally and professionally.

My job as a dog food demonstrator was exactly what I needed and helped get me to the place I was meant to be: living a thriving life.

And if I can fully commit to my passions, so can you.

Try something that is a perfect match to your passions.

~

Try before you buy –
Smartest.
Marketing.
Evah.

~ Donna Fuller

DOG FOOD DIARIES

During my pet food gig, I kept a diary of my daily dealings with the unique animal encounters. Then, using *SantaLand Diaries*, by David Sedaris as my guide, I set out to write a book. I titled it *Dog Food Diaries*. I pictured it as a behind the scenes look at my highly underpaid, yet fulfilling position as a dog food demonstrator.

Soon I learned the hardest part of writing was to sit down and write. I thought it would be easy since I had the notes, but filling a blank page is never easy. Although I knew the concept was something people would love, my brain constantly told me, "No one will read this." Laundry, dirty dishes and organizing my sock drawer suddenly became top priorities. My house had never been cleaner.

Applying the Law of Attraction to other areas of my life had proven beneficial, so I decided to tell myself a new, positive story about my book writing process. My vision was:

> **I have had a good night's sleep and I am ready to sit down and write. God channels the thoughts, ideas, and words through me and they flow easily and effortlessly. I look forward to and enjoy the writing process.**
>
> **First a word, then a sentence, then a paragraph, then another paragraph and before I know it these stories are done!**
>
> **Each day brings me closer to my goal of completing this book. I also use this material for keynote speeches. With each finished story, I feel empowered by my actions and progress and my self-respect and self-esteem soar.**

I read it three times a day, and soon, I found myself spending more time at the keyboard. Eventually, I sat still long enough to write sixty-two stories. Consistency and a positive attitude paid off.

Trying to promote the material as much as possible I posted stories to my website and other sites. I asked my family and friends to read it and even submitted my work to the Erma Bombeck writer's group. No one, including my family and friends, ever gave me feedback. I rationalized, "No news is good news" and hired an editor to review my stories.

When I found someone, the relationship seemed ideal. She barely made any corrections or requested revisions. She was supportive, always telling me, "This is great stuff!" I paid her well to tell me what I wanted to hear.

The red flag should have been when I found myself correcting her mistakes. But my ego said, "best seller" and I started talking to book cover artists and self-publishing companies. I mentioned to a publicist friend of mine, someone who had read some of my stories that I was close to publishing my first book. She said, "Before you go any further, I think my editor friend should give it the once-over." I trusted her judgment and hired another set of eyes.

While writing the book, I had been working through some issues and I was still taking things personally that had happened at the pet store. Apparently, I took my frustrations out on paper, just not as smoothly as David Sedaris.

When I got my submission back the only thing that didn't need revising was the title. The editor said, "There is some really good stuff in here, but it sounds like an angry dog food commercial and I want other people to buy it besides your parents."

Devastated, I cried, "But you don't understand all the freaking work it took to get here. I've gone through job after job settling for comfortable misery because it made everybody else happy. I felt like I was going insane and I wanted out of my life. Finally, and only by the Grace of God, I got myself and my passions figured out and then this job fell into my lap. I've given up nearly everything to stay home and write this. I'm lucky my husband hasn't divorced me!"

Quietly she said, "Well honey, *there's* your book."

In my heart, I knew her feedback was true. But, at that time, I was too disappointed, broke and worn out to bring myself to write another book. I thought about all those poor people who suffered through the first one, but were afraid to tell me it stunk. I refused to put anyone through that again. I threw *Dog Food Diaries* in a drawer and tucked the new book idea away until I could think about it without having a panic attack.

Still, all was not lost. Writing *Dog Food Diaries* had given me valuable experience. I changed my perspective and I gained a positive attitude. I had finished what I started no matter how hard it was. That consistency and persistence would keep me moving forward.

My ego (<u>e</u>dging <u>G</u>od <u>o</u>ut) can be convincing and deceiving and I need to keep it in check. If I had listened to the voice that said "best seller" it would have cost me more to try and sell a book that stunk than what I spent for another set of eyes.

I discovered revisions were humbling, but necessary, to make a piece of art stronger and get my message to my audience. It took creativity, discipline and focus to write the thing. It took courage to put myself out there and face rejection. And it took faith to be willing to try it again.

My job writing *Dog Food Diaries* allowed me to take my knowledge and stories and create humorous, award-winning speeches. It allowed me to continue supporting the cause of being a good pet parent and it helped get me to the place I was meant to be: living a thriving life.

And if I can overcome my inner critic to achieve a goal, so can you.

FOUR PAWS EDU

In spite of the stories in *Dog Food Diaries* not working as a book, I knew my content was solid. I just had to tone things down a bit. I attended a motivational speaking event and watched speakers come alive on stage and capture the audience's attention. It inspired me to be a motivational speaker.

I decided to salvage my funniest stories, combine them with my knowledge, and write an article on pet education. I submitted it to a local newspaper. The article didn't make the cut, but the editor said it was funny and filled with helpful information.

That's all I needed to hear.

From that article, I created four comedy-based speeches on taking care of pets; nutrition, training and safety. I wanted to speak for the pets. I wanted to be their voice. I wanted to continue supporting the cause of being a good pet parent and I knew humor would help get my message across.

I tested the speeches at different Toastmasters meetings. I got rave reviews and won some humor awards. People loved the pet stories and information, so I pulled out my best stuff and created a presentation for the rest of the world to hear. I called it Four Paws Edu.

I made a list of animal people groups and I created a cold-calling script. For practice, I set out to book twenty civic organizations. Naysayers warned me, "It'll take you forever to get that many clubs." Within seven days, I booked twenty clubs.

For the next three months, I waltzed across central Texas connecting with other animal people. I taught them to provide exceptional care, helped them strengthen the bond with their pets and made audiences laugh. I handed out suggestions for high quality, convenient and affordable pet foods telling them, "I don't think your food has to cost as much as college tuition."

My stories and passion won them over. At the end of each gig, they gave me standing ovations and rushed the stage like groupies. I loved connecting with animal people, but I was still too defensive and often used a steamroller approach in sharing my passion.

And, I was stuck on how to make money doing this. I didn't have a "best seller" book that would convince people to hire me to speak for them and I couldn't afford to work for free anymore. I realized I didn't want to be the Critter Whisperer, so I decided to expand my vision.

Again, I saw how no effort was wasted. My first attempt at becoming a motivational speaker and humorist won accolades. I wrote, practiced and tested my material in front of audiences and it gave me confidence on stage. I put myself out there and faced rejection. I asked for and got constructive feedback from a wide variety of pet-friendly people.

It was an opportunity to put the business part of speaking into practice. I targeted an audience and sold myself. I learned pet-friendly people were just the right audience for me.

The experience proved that I had something valuable to offer. This was clear because I was no longer willing to give away my knowledge and services for free. I believed I could be successful as a motivational speaker.

My job speaking on Four Paws Education helped me get to the place I was meant to be: living a thriving life.

And if I can market my skills, so can you.

FOUR PAWS DELI

Dealing with the Bridezillas in my wedding business had convinced me I'd rather cook for dogs. At least the dogs would not complain. I took what I learned about high-quality ingredients in pet food, combined them with my love for cooking and dogs and created two recipes for fresh meat dog treats.

I bought dog bone cookie cutters and heart-shaped mini muffin trays. Then I dusted off my old wedding cake pans and put them to good use. The recipes I created were Pooch Lover Pâté and Liver Lover Muffins. My tagline: *Your dog will stalk you for them!*

I knew the treats would be a great compliment to my Four Paws Edu program. I named my company Four Paws Deli, opening up for business on National Dog Treat Day. My marketing plan entailed selling my treats at the back of the room when speaking and at farmer's markets and craft festivals. Eventually, I hoped to put them into pet stores.

I was familiar with other treats and many were a recipe for paste; flour and water that tasted like chicken. Mine would be all-natural and healthy with *select* ingredients. I knew the holistic health route wasn't cheap, and $20 for an eight-ounce bag wouldn't cut it in retail.

To reduce cost, I bought everything in bulk. My upright freezer was packed full of chicken livers and hearts. I stacked fifty-pound sacks of flaxseed, oats and wheat flour in my extra shower. Because slow cooking the ingredients preserved the nutrition, I usually had three crock-pots going at once, baking sweet potatoes, livers, and hearts.

In the beginning, the treats gave my test dummies gas so badly that nobody was allowed to strike a match near them. I spoke with a veterinarian at Texas A&M who specialized in pet nutrition about my flatulence dilemma. Although he was impressed with my ingredient list, he told me to go easy on the sweet taters. I did and the fumes faded.

I researched colors for my treat bags, logo, and uniform. I wanted people to recognize my brand as easily as they would a can of Coca-Cola. I chose a Kraft brown for my bag (and tent) to give it a natural, homemade look. I went with a blood red for the paw-heart logo and label border trim, so the bag would catch the eye. The bone that went through the red heart and lettering was chocolate brown, because I look good in chocolate brown.

In order to sell the health benefits of the treats, I created an information board displaying colored pictures of the select ingredients. I made everything as eye-catching as possible to make a lasting impression.

I purposely set up camp at the Georgetown, Texas market because when I spoke to the retirees at their RV and pet club, they gave me a standing ovation. Many confessed they wished they'd had pets instead of kids.

I hauled my tent, old wine/pet food card table, and red table cloth to the markets and festivals so I could meet with people face-to-face. I knew getting in front of pet lovers would allow them to feel my energy and passion for my product and for their pets. I handed out free treat samples so customers could "try before they buy". Most times, if the dog scarfed it down, I had a sale.

I built trusted relationships with other vendors. We talked about improving business and using their homegrown products in my treats. Often, with the natural meat companies, I traded dog treats for soup bones for my dogs. From my tent, I helped sell their products and they returned the favor.

I poured thought, effort, and dedication into the business. I thoroughly enjoyed cooking and doing something healthy for the dogs. It was fun connecting with other pet lovers and teaching about being a good pet parent.

Even though I believed in my product and there were days I did well, I learned selling my own stuff was hard. When faced with rejection, I found myself selling customers more on premium dog food than on my own dog treats! I was disappointed, worn out, and broke. Once again, I decided a job with a steady paycheck was the answer.

I learned valuable lessons along the way. I recognized the importance of consistency when creating and marketing a brand and I continued to improve my speaking, people and sales skills.

I knew I wanted to work in the same industry where I could continue supporting the cause of being a good pet parent. Up to this point, I had been focused on promoting healthy lives. Next, I would focus on saving them.

My job making treats at the Four Paws Deli helped get me to the place I was meant to be: living a thriving life.

And if I can refine my mission and seek a job that engages me, so can you.

Seek out jobs that engage you.

~ Donna Fuller

DOG TRAINER

While I was selling pet food, I got pretty good at selling dog training classes for the pet stores. I connected with pet parents and promoted healthy living.

Selling training classes came easily because I knew from experience how an untrained puppy makes you want to pull your hair out. Mine were so rotten, they thought their names were Dammit-Dog, Stop-That, and Get-Over-Here.

I understood that the number one reason there were a bazillion dogs in animal shelters and euthanized each year was a lack of training. Dog training eased the stress of dealing with a crazy puppy. Dog training strengthened the human animal bond between pet and parent, making it less likely for them to end up in a shelter. Dog training saved lives.

I was sure dog training would be a great fit for me, so I looked for work with that purpose in mind. My own therapy would continue because I would love on all sorts of sweet critters.

Part-time work would give me structure, ease me back into the work force and bring me steady income. I could then take my certification anywhere and, best of all, my own dogs would learn to listen-maybe.

I told myself if you can teach angry, hormonal, at-risk teenagers, you can teach dog training. Oddly enough, I found a position available in the small town where I lived.

Red Flag #1:

I went in three different times because I was told to follow up with three different managers. I felt like a kid stuck between my parents; they never gave me a straight answer.

Management wouldn't talk to each other and they refused to return my calls.

I never worked so hard to get a $9.00 an hour job in all my life. And the more work it seemed, the more my gut told me, "Are you sure you want to work for these people?" Desperate to have a steady paycheck and avoid driving to Austin, I dismissed the warning signs and went in for a third time.

I walked straight up to the manager and said, "Look. I've come in here three times, I've spoken to every manager and nobody calls me back. I am competent. I show up for work. I am experienced in the pet industry. I will make you a ton of money. Are you going to hire me or not?"

He looked at me and said, "One question, is there anything you *won't* do?"

"Yep, I don't do rats or reptiles," I answered.

He said, "Okay. Can you start Monday?"

Red Flag #2:

When I told my friend how much work it took to get the job, she said, "Are you sure you want to work for those people?"

Red Flag #3:

I was ready to train dogs, sell premium dog food and save lives!

"When will my training begin?" I asked. "Right now," a manager said, and they sent me to the break room to learn how to train dogs, *online.*

I said, "You know, I'm more of a hand's on kind of gal. Don't I get to work with a real trainer, real animals?"

"Soon," was their automatic response. A couple of weeks before Thanksgiving, they told me, "We could *really* use your help at the cash register."

Reluctantly I agreed, telling myself I'm here to serve and while I am up there I can convert people over to premium dog food and pre-sell classes. In appreciation for my willingness to work the register, or more likely to keep me from walking, they handed me the instructor's dog training manual. I felt like I'd been handed the first edition of the Bible.

Trying to contain my giddiness, I said, "I'll just go to the break room to study." Management said, "Oh no, you study the manual from behind the register." The checkout line stayed backed up for the next six weeks and my training was put on indefinite hold. Still, I kept to my purpose and up sold pet food, pet supplies, and training as much as possible from behind the register.

During their holiday charity collection event, my energy and passion kicked in and I collected more donations for the local animal shelter than anyone had done in the history of the company. Management cheered each time I put a new donation sticker on the wall, but I knew if I was too good behind the cash register I'd end up there for good.

Red Flag #101:

One day, a trainer who worked there before me came through the checkout. She asked, "Have they trained you yet?" I hedged, "No. It's been busy. They'll get to it." She said, "Uh huh. Good luck with that," and walked out the door.

Red Flag #469:

After the holidays they scheduled me to work the cash register for two more weeks. Managers refused to look me in the eye or initiate conversation about anything. I knew my competent cash register skills had paid off; I was stuck there for good and I wouldn't be training dogs anytime soon.

At that point, I thought getting fired would be better than deciding to quit. Every time a new puppy came in, I called for back up and went out on the floor. I was determined to do what I came there to do; help people with their pets.

One day, two new boxer puppies came in with their parents. I called for back up and went out on the floor. We loaded their cart with the works: premium food, new beds, toys, collars, leashes and training classes. As I checked them out, I felt the manager hovering over my shoulder. I knew I was in trouble.

She said, "You can't deviate away from the register anymore."

Fed up, I replied, "I am not on a leash. You watch how far away I deviate from this register."

After several sleepless nights, I decided nine dollars an hour was not worth it. The next morning, I handed them my uniform and my resignation letter. It read, "As promised, I made your company a ton of money. I have been an exceptional employee. You have not followed through as you promised. This is not what I signed up for. My resignation is effective immediately."

I felt empowered and happy that I stood up for myself and immediately applied with their competitor. Before I knew it, managers in several stores fought to hire me. I was clicker-trained immediately at the store I picked. When my energy, passion, and sales skills kicked in, my rooms filled with pet parents at their wits end with their puppies.

In one of my classes, a young man named Jesse brought in Lycan, his four-month-old, German Shepherd puppy. Lycan was the size of a lion, sat like a walrus and thought he was a lap dog. Jesse wanted to take Lycan with him everywhere, but because of his size and strength, it had become near impossible.

We found a private area where I could watch them. Lycan automatically took the lead, pulling Jesse towards the back of the store. And when he saw the wide open aisle, it looked like something out of a cartoon. Lycan was the ski boat going 90-to-nothing. Jesse was the inflatable tube flying behind and holding on for dear life.

After Jesse picked himself up off the floor, I explained, "Lycan doesn't know his own strength. You're thinking, Why does he always ski me through the bark park? While Lycan is thinking, That's the way you walk your human!"

I showed him how to stop the pulling, and then stood back and watched. During the first pass, Jesse tried to walk with him, but Lycan continued to race down the aisle dragging Jesse behind. I saw his embarrassment and excused myself, giving them some privacy.

I went down another aisle and spied on them from around the corner. By the third pass, Lycan still walked like a lion, but this time right by Jesse's side. They both looked up at me and grinned from ear to ear. For the first time, they understood how to walk each other.

Dog training ain't about training the dog. The dogs were the easy part. Humans were more resistant to learning new tricks because they were afraid of looking dumber than the dog.

Usually by the second class, they saw results and were more open to learning. With weekly sessions, stress levels at home decreased while the respect for and understanding of one another increased. By graduation, the human animal bond was solid and lives were saved.

I worked that job like a dog's life depended on it, and it served its purpose. I loved on all those sweet critters for my therapy. The structure eased me back into the workforce and brought me steady income. I improved my speaking and sales skills in front of the right audience and in the right industry.

I was on the right path for me. I discovered my passion and gained valuable experience in jobs that were a great fit. However, I saw a pattern. I got hired and was an exceptional employee. I made the company's profits explode. Everyone was happy, but me. No one wanted to pay me for the passion, energy, experience and value I brought to the table.

Then it hit me. During this process, not only had I realized my passions I had realized my worth. I knew I wanted a job that allowed me to continue supporting the cause of being a good pet parent *and* paid me my worth. That job had to be out there.

Dog training taught me invaluable lessons in behavior. I learned how to create a positive, well-timed association with others. I learned how to effectively increase a desired behavior and to reward that behavior. And last, I learned the importance of staying consistent.

The only thing I didn't learn was how to get my own dogs to listen.

The lessons I learned in my job as a dog trainer would catapult my career to a level I never imagined possible. It helped get me to the place I was meant to be: living a thriving life.

And if I can recognize my worth, so can you.

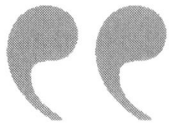

*Everything learned in
dog training can be used on
your husband, your children,
your customers,
and yourself.*

~ Donna Fuller

DOG DRUG DEALER

I didn't want just any job. I wanted a job where I could stay true to my passion and get paid my worth. My gut said that job existed. My gut said I'd find it. I just wasn't sure what it was.

Even though I had built credibility and solid sales numbers in an industry I loved, old fears and habits kicked in. I felt desperate and began applying for every kind of job I could find, whether it was a good fit or not. Thankfully, I got no responses.

Then, it dawned on me, we bring about what we think about, so I decided to create an ideal job vision. I believed, with God's help in creating my vision, I could increase my chances of getting the perfect job.

With that in mind I wrote everything down that I wanted from my new job, no matter how far-fetched. This is what God and I came up with:

JOB VISION

Employer: Fun, respectful, and family-oriented. Sees my worth and pays me for my skills.
Willing to invest in me.
Opportunity for growth.
Service-oriented.

Dress: Business casual to casual.

Benefits: Affordable health benefits.
3-week vacation.
Holidays and sick leave.
Paid training.

Hire date: End of September.

I was inspired to FOCUS: Follow One Course Until Successful. I read over my vision each morning and again before I went to sleep. I soon began to see myself having my ideal job. I still wasn't getting any nibbles when I sent out my resume, but I had faith the job would come and match my vision.

Next, I was encouraged to take a free LinkedIn class. Mind you, I knew nothing about it and am technically challenged, but I set up my profile anyway. As a result of the profile creation process, I recognized new marketable skills. I had a steady work history and great sales numbers in the field. I was resourceful and took initiative. I was personable, funny and knew how to take excellent care of customers. I knew how to kick tail and take names.

It became clear to me that being a drug rep for veterinarians would be a dream job. Then the naysayers, many of them in own head, shouted, "It will take you forever to land a job like that." I listened to my gut instead. My gut said stay focused. My gut said this is the right direction. My gut said this is the match to your vision.

While surfing through LinkedIn profiles, I looked for people with similar job titles and asked them for informal interviews. I stuck with people outside my region (and state) so no one would think I was after their job.

Mid-September, I found an animal health manager in California. He generously gave me an hour of his time. We talked about his background and career path. We talked about my background and sales successes. In the end I confessed, "I just want you to hire me."

He said, "Here's what I suggest you do. Find the closest veterinarian conference and attend. Most hiring managers in the pet industry will be there and you can make some connections."

Immediately, I searched for veterinarian conferences online. It turned out the SW Veterinary Symposium would be held in San Antonio, just 3 days away. I knew to get hired I'd have to get in front of people. They had to see me in action, feel my passion and energy or I'd be just another resume at the bottom of the stack.

I paid $75 for an Exhibitor's hall pass. I wanted them to remember my face so I made business cards that included my professional mug shot. Armed with resumes and business cards, I drove two hours determined to land my ideal job.

On the drive down, I created and memorized an elevator pitch. Dressed to kill, I walked into the hall and confidently went from booth to booth asking for the hiring manager and giving them my pitch. I handed out fifteen resumes and had four sit-down interviews on the spot.

I got a great job. I felt blessed because I could check off almost everything on my job vision. I missed my end of September deadline but considered October 10th, close enough.

The first two weeks of my on-the-job-training consisted of wandering around the warehouse familiarizing myself with a bazillion different drugs and pet supplies or listening to vendor after vendor detail their products. It was always the same spiel, "There's no other product out there like it."

The one time things got interesting was when a pet food vendor tried convincing me that his product didn't contain roadkill. When he realized I knew differently, things turned ugly and I came close to getting fired over a bag of pet food. I refused to sell something I didn't believe in. In the end, we agreed to disagree, and I kept my job.

The last week of training I spent three full days in a car with my boss. I thought I don't even want to be in a car with Maverick that long, and I like him. My boss tried to prove to me that he still "had it", so we hit twelve to sixteen clinics a day. There was no balance. I was exhausted and I got very crabby. I was more than ready to start working on my own, so he cut me loose.

I soon learned my new territory was damaged. I was warned it would be hard to get customers back. The girl who had the job before me had thought the way to do business was to cuss like a sailor and share intimate details about her sex life within ear shot of the vet clinic's customers.

The heads-up spurred me to prove them wrong. I set out to make new friends, build customer's trust and take care of them like nobody's business. I used my dog training knowledge on my customers because dog training ain't about training the dog.

Considering my audience, I dressed like a cowgirl. I wore starched button-down shirts, jeans, and boots. My best investment was my blingy, rhinestone belt. Damage control in a competitive field required me to stand out and create a positive association. I knew they might not remember my name, but they were going to remember that belt.

The strategy worked so well, they called me "the girl with the blingy belt". Everyone knew who they were talking about and other reps started dressing like me.

To reward my customers for doing business

with me, I brought them fresh strawberries and healthy lunches to sustain them throughout their busy day. For Father's day I passed out 162 batches of homemade banana pudding. I treated my customers like royalty and they stayed loyal.

I took ownership in their practice needs and bent over backward solving their problems. I researched which products would save and make them money. I was an advocate for quality products and used my test-dummies at home to give product feedback. It was part of my Honest-Abe philosophy.

I made friends with other reps, never seeing them as "the enemy". Those good relationships came in handy, especially when I didn't carry what my customer needed. It was important for me to get the customer's needs met.

One day, on the way to Mexia, I saw some people running across the busy highway. They were waving at oncoming traffic to stop or slow down. As I approached the scene, I saw one very scared donkey running loose across the highway.

I threw on my flashers, pulled over, and yelled, "How can I help?"

Cars were flying by. One of the men pointed

towards an open gate, where I saw several donkeys ready to make their escape. Seven dogs were out on the side of the road watching the people run up and down the highway. I parked in front of the entrance hoping to distract the animals by blocking their view while I got them back inside the fence.

I grabbed my bag of dog treats from the front seat of my car, shook the bag at everybody and instantly became a star. I shooed the donkeys back from the fence and lured all the dogs back in.

I shut the gate and began walking up the highway to see how else I could help. Other people had stopped to help corral the terrified donkey, but several times she tried to dart back across the highway.

I thought I would make myself useful by stopping or slowing traffic. I had the bright idea of stepping out into the highway when I thought oncoming cars were far enough away. I felt invisible because few people slowed down until they were right on top of the scene. I got a lot of flipped birds until startled drivers realized what was happening and that I wasn't just some lunatic out playing in traffic.

Since my hazard lights didn't seem to help much, I decided I needed something bright and shiny to grab their attention. I unbuckled my blingy belt, pulled it off and held it up like Rocky after he won Heavyweight Champion of the World. The sun reflected off the rhinestones like stadium lights, bringing traffic to a halt. The owners were able to calm the donkey down and bring her safely back home.

Each time I entered a clinic I asked God to help me be of service to my customers. They deserved to be showered with respect, appreciation and generosity and, by God, that's what I was serving. I learned during my power plant days that generosity equaled good karma and when people felt appreciated they wanted to return the favor.

Each month, I sent out handwritten thank you notes to all customers who did business with me; my mother raised me right. However, when I shared my *signature move* with my co-workers and other reps, they balked, saying they didn't have time. By my first year anniversary, I had increased sales by 300%. I enjoyed what I did for the animal clinics and the pets so much it was the only job I would keep doing even if I won the lottery.

But as much as I loved the job, I was back in the same old boat. I was an exceptional employee. I made the company's profits explode. Still, I felt devalued and disrespected because I was not being paid for the passion, energy, experience and value I brought to the table.

To be honest, I knew on day five of my training that the company and I were not a good fit. Regardless, I chose to stay so I could continue to utilize my natural strengths and talents, and support the cause of being a good pet parent. I wanted to build my sales numbers, make connections in the industry and become a successful drug rep. And, I had succeeded.

Even though I got almost everything I asked for from my job vision, it was time to sharpen the focus. I wrote a new vision that included greater details about what was important to me in a company's business philosophy.

I believe in taking care of customers and that you treat your employees like they are your greatest asset. I believe you reward your employees for bringing in revenue and supporting the company's vision. I believe you reward customers for doing business with you. I believe in making friends with the competition. I believe you give to receive because

generosity equals good karma. Most of all, I believe you stay consistent in everything you do.

I wanted to work for someone who had that same business philosophy. And I thought to myself, "That's me!"

I loved taking care of my customers and I felt guilty at the thought of leaving them. During my last year there, I thought about speaking again and started writing a training program to help pet friendly people be successful in customer service.

Despite my success and because of our differing philosophies, my boss decided to fire me. When he did, I told him, "You have done me a HUGE favor." Getting fired didn't make me a failure. I was not okay with their business philosophies. I went home that afternoon and sent out over 200 handwritten notes to all my veterinary clinics thanking them for their business.

That evening I finished writing my new training course centered in the certainty that all I know about customer service, I learned in dog training. I knew I had valuable insight to share that would help employers and employees alike. I solidified my strengths, kept my sense of humor, stayed true to my passion and clarified my vision. Now, I was ready to put my business philosophy into action.

It was a blessing the day he hired me and a blessing the day he fired me. My job as a dog drug dealer helped get me to the place I was meant to be: living a thriving life.

And if I can clarify an ideal vision, so can you.

JOKER

Even though I had always been able to get a laugh, it never occurred to me to do stand-up comedy. I didn't dream about it as a kid. I didn't consider it as a career path because it wasn't a *real* job.

However, humor is my default mode. My brain is wired to see the irony and point out things I find amusing, usually in a mocking tone. I don't have an off-switch. It comes naturally and it comes quickly. I can't control it, even if I wanted to.

I had seen comics that made me laugh till I cried. And I loved how it felt when my sides hurt for a couple days after laughing hard. But it wasn't until I did work on my insides, stayed true to my passions and surrounded myself with furry, four-legged therapists, that I realized

I wanted to be the one to make other people's sides hurt.

All my life I had used humor to defuse situations and save my sanity. I gained acceptance from others and made people laugh. It was a high like no food, money or cocktail had ever brought me. And, it didn't leave me fat, broke or stupid.

During my job at the engineering firm I learned the importance of humor. I kept that in the back of my mind when I gave speeches. When friends encouraged me to test some comedy material at my Toastmasters meetings, I won some Best Humor Awards that I proudly put on my resume (and my mom's fridge).

I knew hanging around funny people would keep my funny juices flowing. I took a couple of comedy classes surrounding myself with like-minded individuals. I collected and read all the books they suggested, did my homework and always came away feeling happy, creative and inspired.

Someone once told me, you'll always get a laugh anytime you speak through the eyes of a pet. Lucky for me, I had plenty of that kind of material, so I used it in our comedy showcase. With 150 people in the audience, I was a nervous wreck. But when I got up on stage, thankfully, I couldn't see anything past the lights.

I got through my set without hyperventilating. Although, it felt like the longest five minutes of my life, I was hooked. The only thing I wasn't hooked on was the late night because my bedtime is 9:30.

A few months later, massive fires blew through the county where we lived threatening our home. Right before we were evacuated, I grabbed the most important things: Maverick, my critters and my computer. I threw mixed items from my office in a tote box. Then I took one last look around the house and thought it's just stuff and anything else I need I can buy at Walmart.

I learned two things from that natural disaster: One, we had way too much stuff. And two, comedy was more important than I realized because when I opened my tote, my comedy and speaking books were the only ones I had grabbed.

A few months later, I had the opportunity to meet with comedian Judy Carter. When I told her it was her book, the *Comedy Bible*, that was one of the only books I saved, she almost cried.

Reluctantly, I shared with some trusted friends that I had dabbled in stand-up comedy. Unanimously, and without hesitation they said, "I can see you doing that." I was flattered. I knew they were right, but I thought, "That's not a *real* job." I went out and found myself one. At least I picked a real job that was a great fit.

Being a drug rep kept me away from my Toastmasters meetings for almost two years and I missed it. When I got the bug to speak again, I stopped by to see my group. My friend, Amy, greeted me at the door, shoved a piece of paper in my hand and ordered, "Fill this out."

I blindly followed her orders thinking, "This must be their new way of getting to know people." Within minutes, they announced me as the next speaker, so I shared about my stand-up comedy experience. The speech was rough, but people laughed and I felt more alive than I had in months.

Amy helped me take the funny stuff from my Four Paws Edu presentation and add it to the training course I had written, tightening it up. A couple months after my drug rep job ended, I was back waltzing across central Texas, training and entertaining company employees in customer service and dog training.

However, I was terrified when I told my business coach that my gut said to dabble in comedy again. I gave her excuse after excuse of why it wouldn't pan out....Not a *real* job...late nights kill me...blah, blah, blah. She threw out "we bring about what we think about" and suggested I write a comedy vision--no matter how far-fetched. Just lay it all out there. Visualize the atmosphere, the audience, your life, everything about this path, the way you want to see it pan out.

When I sat down to write, the vision poured out of me:

I create and perform clean comedy that anyone can enjoy. My muse kicks in, years of material pour out of me and I know there will always be enough. My material is hilarious, useful, clean, and it KILLS! I could be hired by the Pope if I wanted!

I can't wait to make people laugh. I do what it takes to become great because that's what my audience deserves. I am a member of a humor circle and we support and inspire each other. I receive guidance

and direction from experts who show me what to do next because they care about me and my future. I get in the practice time so I am prepared and polished.

Stage sound is clear for me and the crowd. Clapping and laughter echoes through the building as the audience resonates with my material. I look out at the crowd and see people bent over laughing and wiping the tears from their eyes. I well up with appreciation. Time flies by for everyone because we are having so much fun.

I go there to be of service and it's the best way I know how. People need and want funny in their lives.

I am comfortable and conversational on stage. My timing is dead on and my mechanics are smooth. I am fearless. I am competent. I am creative. I am authentic. I am relatable. I am edgy. I am sarcastic. I am self-deprecating.

I decide to do this and everything falls into place quickly because it's what I am supposed to be doing. The offers, the

money come rolling in from all different directions. I am able to give back. Generosity = good Karma. I get the training I need, the right people take notice and I get better and better. I feel fulfilled and this life turns out better than I ever expected.

I put it in an email to my coach and hit send.

Two days later, I reconnected with my old comedy friend, Bob. He was now part of a five-person group called Door to Door Comedy, who went door to door looking for gigs.

Bob said, "We're all older, so we book stuff early. We call one of our members Nine-o-clock-Nora, because she likes to be in bed by nine. Would you like to join our group?"

Shocked, I said, "Sure!"

He said, "Great, but there is one requirement, your material has to be church-clean."

A month later, I was waltzing across central Texas, getting paid to do clean comedy with a circle of humor friends. We performed for Chamber of Commerce events, retirement communities and apartment complexes.

However, one of the most interesting gigs was for a Catholic nursing home.

We walked into a large open room with a Christmas tree, even though it was June. There were only a dozen chairs lined up for the audience. As I thought to myself we should get more chairs, the sisters began wheeling in residents, one after another, until the room was filled with forty or so women. The youngest woman was pushing 85 and a walker. The rest of them had to be pushed.

A resident's aunt warned Nora, "It would help if you could be overly animated and loud, since most of them are half blind and deaf." I looked around the room to see several of them nodding off before the show even started. Things were not looking good.

Some of the residents looked scared, like we would make them suffer through something horrendous. When they realized we were there to entertain them, they relaxed a bit, although some still gave us attitude. One lady spoke up for her clique of women, "We'll go ahead and stay for your "show", but make it quick." Like they could really escape?

The loud microphone woke everyone up and faces began to brighten as Suzanna worked the crowd. She asked for those celebrating birthdays and we sang to them. The oldest turned out to be 102.

Many women owned pets at one time in their lives. There were a few who hadn't yet graduated from independent to assisted living, who still had them. When I did my dog bit, my fellow pet lovers came alive.

In the end, they applauded our show and we made great connections with those who stayed awake long enough. As I perform comedy, I realize how people desperately need humor in their lives. They need to be lifted up and feel happy.

Comedy has taught me that my biggest heckler is in my own mind. It often tells me:

You ain't got nothin'

You don't know nothin'

You ain't nothin'

Talk about a hostile working environment. I don't buy into that kind of badgering as long as I stay clear with my vision. And my vision had to be written so I could keep focusing on it. I may not have seen how it would pan out exactly, but getting clear and putting what I want down in writing, helped speed up the process.

I learned, with practice, my timing and mechanics got better and I became more comfortable and conversational on stage. And best of all, I found out I could do comedy and still be at home by ten.

My job as a comedian strengthened my funny skills and got me to the place I was meant to be: living a thriving life.

And if I can write a clear vision and believe it, so can you.

COMEDIC CATALYST

My presentation, *All I Know about Customer Service I Learned in Dog Training,* was a huge hit. People rushed me like groupies to a stage and businesses were clamoring to hire me to train and entertain their staff.

I loved talking about the dogs and connecting with pet lovers in the audience. I loved helping people succeed in their business. Still, the thought of solely teaching customer service for the next twenty years gave me panic attacks.

It didn't feel right for me, but I brushed my feelings aside telling myself I was just scared. When I started a new book on customer service, it took me four months to write one chapter and I was miserable the whole time. My gut said I was chasing the money instead of my passion and I needed a course correction.

Meanwhile, our comedy group was going strong, so Bob encouraged me to compete in the Clean Comedy Challenge. At first, my ears perked up. Then, I found out it would be held in the middle of an Indiana cornfield, two hours away from civilization. Since I am on the once-every-twelve-year vacation plan, I thought it best to stick to my motto: if traveling more than three hours from home, there better be waves of foam.

I wanted to pick up sea shells, not corn husks.

Then they moved the venue a *little further south* to St. Pete's beach in Florida. Major game changer. I thought... sugar sand beaches... oceans of blue green... and COMEDY. I am so there.

The comedy challenge started on a Wednesday afternoon in July. I walked into the Coconuts Comedy Club with 15 other comics at all stages of the game. Slight tension and nervous forced jokes filled the air, but soon we relaxed and became funny friends for life.

COMEDIC CATALYST

Here is how the week's agenda broke down. Comedy veterans with over twenty years of experience taught afternoon workshops. Then, we broke for dinner. At 9 p.m. we hit the comedy stage to perform our first set. Every set was judged by a professional comedian and the next day we received a private evaluation from them.

The whole trip, I took care of myself and stayed replenished. I didn't go to the Waffle House after each show. I took early morning walks on the beach. I prayed and meditated. I got a massage and took naps. I took a risk, chased my passions and did what set my heart on fire.

And, each night I got up on stage and provided unconditional service to the audience. Just like my dogs taught me.

Most comics might consider going up second in the line-up the kiss of death. Not me, I was about to hyperventilate and wanted it to be over.

After my set, judge Bill Gordo gave me some advice. He said, "To calm your nerves, jump up and down 100 times and down a shot of caffeine." I'm a good listener, the next night before my set I ran a marathon and downed a six-pack of Diet Mountain Dew.

Good thing, because comedy legend Eddie Brill was judging. For seventeen years he booked for David Letterman. In late night television, Eddie Brill was considered a comedy god and his word the gospel. I went up on stage, did my set and gave it my best shot. The next day Brill led our workshop and gave us our evaluations.

He told our group, "You might struggle in the beginning because you're not sure who you are yet." And that is when he looked at me and said, "You came out on stage, you were really funny and I'll point it out in front of everyone, you have *it*."

I looked behind me to see who on earth he was talking to. Realizing he meant me, I was flattered and a bit embarrassed, especially for him, because I knew at any moment he would turn and say, "Sorry, I thought you were somebody else."

When I walked in for my personal evaluation with him, he said, "I already gave you your feedback."

I said, "Good, because I got it on tape, so you can't take it back. And while you're at it, *define it*."

Showing me his notes he said, "Look... good personality on stage. You can tell you love it...

COMEDIC CATALYST

You have what it takes to be a performer. You have what it takes to be a comedian. Now you just have to do the hard stuff, the writing. So write, write, write. But natural, very funny. You can't buy that."

On the plane ride home, and for several weeks after, I listened to my evaluation over and over, grinning from ear to ear. You might think the success of the trip was due to his feedback. Although that was an exciting, unexpected perk, the success was because I stayed true to myself.

Thinking back about the classes and the friends I made, I realized the trip taught me to know my limits. I couldn't even do comedy on a senior cruise ship because my bedtime is at 9:30pm! It was clear I needed to be funny during banker's hours.

I went to my writing friend, Anne, for advice. I knew speaking about customer service and writing a book about it was not the path for me. I knew comedy was the path for me. Now that I knew I had *it,* it was time to figure out what I was meant to do with *it.*

She asked, "Whatever happened to your book, *Dog Food Diaries?*"

I told her about my disappointment and embarrassment from the editor's feedback.

Then I said, "And you have no idea what it took to get here. I went through job after job, settling for comfortable misery, because it made everybody else happy. I felt like I was going insane and I wanted out of my life. Finally, and only by the Grace of God, I got myself and my passions figured out and I've been moving forward ever since. I am so close I can feel it. All I want to do is to make people laugh. All I want to do is to help people get to the place they are meant to be. Because if *I* can do it..."

Quietly, she said, "Well, *there's* your book."

I said, "You're the second person to tell me that."

"Are you gonna wait for a third?" she asked.

If you are reading this book, you know my answer was no. I sat down and reluctantly made a list of all my *real* jobs. The number was staggering. I almost swallowed my gum.

But I knew, no matter if I held the job for a day or for seven years, they all had value. Each job offered me an opportunity to grow and learn. I knew those lessons could be helpful to others. And, hilarious.

So I sat down and wrote another vision:

God has given me this incredible gift

and I use it to the fullest extent. I write this book for the reader. God shows me what to write and say. I am here to serve others.

Writing the book and keynote speech are easy and they jive. The short stories are a fun and quick read. The lessons are easy to grasp. I giggle through the process of making others laugh.

The audience gets exactly what they need and want. The book adds value to their lives. It makes them think. It makes them laugh. It makes them feel better. It makes their lives better. My stories and lessons motivate others to take inspired action.

I believe in myself. I believe in my God-given talents. I trust my creative abilities. I live the abundant, ah-mazing, prosperous life that God has in store for me. I believe in my ability to help others do the same. I am here to serve others.

This job has taught me it is possible to do clean comedy in the daylight and to share what I've learned while doing it. I need to do what sets my heart on fire and then figure out ways to turn my passions into profits.

I have to make sure it's a good fit for me and to take care of myself. Sometimes, that goes against the norm of a late night trip to the Waffle House. Sometimes, it means ignoring what everyone else is doing to do things my way.

My job as a funny motivational speaker is my real job. I am meant to help people live healthy, happy and engaged lives. I am meant to help people thrive in life.

And if I can stay true to myself, so can you.

THE END

All of our resumes are combinations of stories and lessons. I warned you, mine's colorful, and this isn't even the half of it. I think I've done it all. Well, I haven't danced on tables. Not for money anyway.

But, each job helped me recognize and strengthen my natural abilities and instincts. Each job trained me to be better in the next one. Each job got me to the place I am today.

This book was about what I did and learned. And by no means am I saying you have to leave your current job to find your passions, purpose or yourself. Shoot, you might already be in the right spot. Still, I thought I would end it with a vision—my ideal vision for *you:*

You recognize your God-given talents and strengths. You make choices that are a good fit for you. You utilize your skills and gifts to the fullest extent. You do what you enjoy and come alive.

You find the humor in your life. You persevere because you don't take life so seriously. You keep your sense of humor and you keep your sanity.

You take time to nourish and care for your mind and body. You slow down and give yourself time to decompress. You do things that soothe your soul so you open up to discover, or rediscover, what sets your heart on fire.

You find your passions. You go toward your passions. You do not settle for less. Your passions lead you to your purpose. Your let passion guide you to how to best serve others. You DO what sets your heart on fire.

You put your vision to paper-no matter how far-fetched. And you make it ideal. You see you are worth it. You see you

THE END

deserve it. You watch your super powers kick in and your vision turns into reality.

You choose to think positive thoughts. You choose to take positive action. You exert positive energy in everything you do, because you are happy, healthy and engaged in life.

Country star Reba McIntyre said:

**To thrive in life you need 3 kinds of bones:
A wishbone; A backbone;
And a funny bone - my favorite part
of the bird.**

We are meant to thrive. Let's do it with humor, passion, vision and positive energy. Only when we thrive, can we fully serve others.

And isn't that the true meaning of success?

No matter how they panned out, each of my seventy-one jobs (no joke) was an opportunity to learn, laugh and grow.

I hope you will take what I learned and get to the place you were *all* meant to be, living a thriving life.

And if I can do it, so can you.

*Let your passion
be your guide
to how you can
better serve others.*

~ Donna Fuller

ACKNOWLEDGEMENTS

My mom: I appreciate your dry wit and the restraint it takes to butt out; especially when I made poor choices in life. And for having the patience of Mother Teresa.

My dad: I appreciate you teaching me about honesty, integrity and serving others. And how to count back change, a skill rarely used these days.

And to the both of you for being there **all-the-time**.

Judi, my other mom: I appreciate the excitement you have for me each time I start a new adventure.

Dardi: I appreciate your support and for telling me when my butt looked fat. And for staying my friend, even when common sense probably told you different.

Laughing Matters Toastmasters Club: I appreciate the fun meetings and your gentle, encouraging feedback.

Door to Door Comedy: I appreciate you toughing it out while I built up confidence and worked the kinks out of my comedy.

Suzanna Brown: I appreciate you helping me start this book. You is one creative cookie.

Melissa Roth: I appreciate you helping me finish this book. You fit my editor vision perfectly.

Coach Dallman: I hope you know from above that swim team years were some of the best in my life, even if I stunk.

I appreciate all the people who ever worked with me when I was not in the right place and out of my right mind.

My Grampa Fuller: You were my saving grace. And I know it was you who sent my dogs to save me, again.

INDEX

4

4th of July 30, 32

A

abilities 25, 201, 203
artists 60, 149
attention span 70
attitude .. 41, 42, 149, 151, 192
attorney 54
Austin 45, 50, 75, 165

B

babysitters 17
Baskin-Robbins . 27, 29, 30, 32, 60
big city 43, 75
Bridezillas 63, 157
Brill, Eddie 198
business cards ... 58, 59, 61, 62, 63, 176

C

cake decorator 61
cakes 60, 61, 70
camaraderie 32

character......................... 4, 127
Christmas 7, 50, 91, 192
Clean Comedy Challenge .. 196
Clear Springs Café 38, 41
Coconuts Comedy Club..... 196
cold calls 23
comedy. 73, 153, 185, 186, 187, 188, 189, 191, 193, 194, 196, 197, 198, 199, 201, 208, 215
Comedy Bible 187
Correcaminos...................... 22
customers. 3, 10, 11, 17, 18, 29, 30, 37, 38, 44, 45, 46, 133, 135, 139, 141, 142, 144, 159, 160, 175, 178, 181, 182, 183

D

Dallmann, Coach........... 22, 24
Damage control 178
day-care 13
Dog Food Diaries 145, 147, 151, 153, 199
drive... 25, 66, 85, 92, 117, 176

E

empowered 36, 38, 42, 55, 87, 125, 144, 148, 168

exhilaration......................... 38
Eyes of Texas 68

F

failure 47, 48, 183
faith 63, 113, 151, 175
fearless ... 66, 69, 97, 111, 117, 190
fears........... 111, 114, 120, 173
fired 43, 47, 57, 60, 63, 167, 177, 183, 184
focus ... 45, 116, 119, 151, 161, 182
football 68
Forrest Gump 24
Fuller, Grampa 1, 3, 208

G

garage sales 5, 7, 8, 11
generosity 181, 183
Gibb, Andy 2
God 38, 40, 57, 63, 76, 77, 118, 145, 148, 150, 151, 173, 174, 181, 200, 201, 204
good fit . 47, 48, 64, 66, 67, 72, 92, 173, 182, 202, 204
Gruene Dolphins................. 22

INDEX

H

habits 173
happiness 97, 99
heckling 40
Hooters 45
humor . 32, 33, 72, 73, 83, 119, 131, 154, 184, 185, 186, 189, 191, 193, 204, 205, 215

I

ideal vision 184, 204
integrity 48, 129, 144, 207
interviews 175, 177
irony 185

K

karma 181, 183

L

Letterman, David 198
LinkedIn 175
Longhorns 68

M

marketing plan 61, 158
McIntyre, Reba 205
Mexico City 22
motivated 24, 40
motivational 28, 153, 155, 156, 202, 215
motivational speaker 153, 155, 156, 202, 215

N

nail tech 60

P

parties 58, 59
party planning 59
passions 42, 100, 110, 111, 119, 131, 144, 145, 150, 171, 185, 197, 200, 202, 203, 204
perfect job 174
perseverance 25, 32
persevere 32, 33, 204
philosophy 4, 144, 179, 182, 183, 184
planning . 58, 59, 60, 61, 62, 88
police 59, 60

protection 63
public speaking 35

R

real job 27, 28, 59, 65, 79, 185, 188, 189, 202
receptionist 65, 70
recovery 66
rejection 23, 63, 133, 151, 155, 160
respect .. 18, 48, 69, 71, 86, 92, 93, 128, 137, 148, 170, 181
resumes 176, 177, 203

S

samples 61, 62, 159
self-confidence 32
self-sufficiency 18
signs 9, 48, 63, 100, 165
skills 4, 5, 11, 18, 37, 40, 41, 85, 88, 90, 92, 99, 124, 137, 139, 156, 160, 167, 168, 170, 174, 175, 194, 204
stamina 25
success 18, 118, 183, 199, 205, 215
swim team 21
Swim-a-thon 22, 23, 24, 25

swimming 22, 25, 83

T

talents. 4, 18, 41, 63, 182, 201, 204
Texas. 1, 2, 3, 4, 29, 50, 58, 63, 68, 141, 154, 158, 159, 188, 191, 215
thriving x, 4, 11, 19, 25, 33, 42, 48, 55, 64, 73, 84, 93, 101, 112, 120, 129, 138, 145, 152, 156, 161, 171, 184, 194, 205
tip 39, 40
tips 37
Toastmasters 98, 113, 116, 119, 121, 137, 154, 186, 188, 208
Twilight Zone 61

U

upselling 38

V

vegetable stand 1, 3, 4, 10, 140
veterinarian 80, 158, 176
vision 11, 83, 84, 122, 129,

INDEX

148, 155, 173, 174, 175, 177, 182, 184, 189, 193, 194, 200, 203, 204, 205, 208

vulnerable 54, 128

W

waitress . 36, 38, 42, 43, 48, 71

wedding 57, 58, 60, 61, 62, 64, 90, 109, 157

Find your passions.

*Put your passions
on the front burner.*

*Do what sets
your heart on fire.*

~ Donna Fuller

ABOUT THE AUTHOR

Donna Fuller uses her super powers for good as a funny motiva-tional speaker, comedian and coach. Although her work history is *diverse*, her passion for pets brought her great success in the animal health industry.

Today, Donna entertains and trains audiences to be happy, healthy and engaged at work and at home-she teaches people how to thrive in life.

She has won several humor awards for her speeches and stand-up comedy routines.

Donna and her husband, Maverick, live in a barn on 45 acres in Texas, with all their critters.

Read something funny or uplifting before you drift off at night.

Go to sleep thinking positive thoughts.

*No news.
No Walking Dead.
– after 6 p.m.*

~ Donna Fuller

CONTACT DONNA

Donna speaks humorously on the topic of personal transformation and work life balance. She works with organizations that want happy, healthy and engaged employees at work and at home.

Happy Work. Happy Life. An Inside Job. is the companion book to her keynote speech.

Donna can deliver a keynote or half-day version of this content that will train and entertain your audience. If you are interested in finding out more please contact her at:

www.fullerhumor.com

Email:
dfuller@fullerhumor.com

Live like somebody left the gate open!

~ Somebody really smart

THRIVE

T: Tap Into Your Super Powers
H: Handle Life With Humor
R: Replenish - Take Time to Replenish
I: Ignite Your Passions
V: Vision - Create Your Ideal Vision
E: Exert Positive Energy

Made in the USA
Charleston, SC
28 August 2015